The Arabs

The Arabs

Maxime Rodinson

Translated by

Arthur Goldhammer

The University of Chicago Press

MAXIME RODINSON is Directeur d'Etudes at l'Ecole practique
des hautes études at the Sorbonne.

Originally published as *Les Arabes*, © 1979 by Presses Universitaires de France.

The University of Chicago Press, Chicago 60637
Croom Helm, Ltd., London

©1981 by The University of Chicago and
Croom Helm, Ltd.
All rights reserved. Published 1981
Printed in the United States of America

85 84 83 82 81   5 4 3 2 1

Library of Congress Cataloging in Publication Data

Rodinson, Maxime.
    The Arabs.

    Translation of Les Arabes.
    Includes index.
    1. Arabs.   I. Title.
DS36.7.R6213   909'.04927   80–25916
ISBN 0–226–72355–0
ISBN 9–226–72356–9 (pbk.)

Contents

Contents

*A Note on the Transliteration
and Pronunciation of Arabic*

The macron distinguishes long vowels from short vowels. Arabic vowels are "pure," i.e., pronounced with uniform quality as in Italian or Spanish, not with a "glide" into a *w* or *y* sound as in many dialects of English; the following equivalents are therefore only approximate.

a as in *bat*; *ā* variously as in *sand, dart,* or *call.*

i as in *bit*; *ī* as in *beat.*

u as in *pull, put* (not as in *but*); *u* as in *pool, boot.* The diagraphs *sh* and *th* represent the same sounds as in English.

dh is the voiced equivalent of *th* (*this,* as opposed to *thin*).

kh is the velar fricative of Scottish *loch* or German *ach.*

gh is its voiced equivalent (something like a gargle, or an exaggerated French *r grasséyé* as in *rarement*).

h is a velar *h,* similar to Spanish *j* as in *bajo,* but produced farther back.

q is similar to *k,* but produced farther back on the palate.

The apostrophe ' represents a glottal stop, as heard between the words *Alva Edison* clearly articulated, or in the Cockney *lil bo'ls*. The sign ' represents a guttural "squeezing" of the breath through the constricted throat.

Subscript dots are used to distinguish four so-called 'emphatic' consonants ($ḍ$, $ṣ$, $ṭ$, $ẓ$), which are pronounced with the middle of the tongue raised toward the palate.

All other consonants (including h, j, w, z) are pronounced more or less as in English.

Conventional English forms of geographical names and technical terms are used where these exist.

➤ Preface ◄

Can anyone claim to be utterly without interest in the Arab people—even if it takes some spectacularly newsworthy event to arouse that interest? And it hardly needs mentioning that over the past two or three decades there have been more and more such events, until one seems to merge into the next in an almost continuous series. And who can claim that the Arabs never figure in his conversation—for most of us are quite ready to form opinions and pass judgment without having all the facts in hand. Indeed, the Arabs themselves have for some time now been apt to argue their own case more than can be explained merely by that interest in one's own fate that all men share.

Yet ignorance is as prevalent as discussion. The specialist—who deserves no special credit for his comparatively detailed and accurate knowledge, which must in any case be weighed against his many blind spots—is often chagrined when he hears or reads statements that are erroneous or at any rate so crude as to be inaccurate or distorted by insertion in a misleading context. Add to this the inevitable twisting of the facts by passion, whether overt or concealed (we shall be forced to revert to this question of passion later on). Indeed, at this moment in history, the Arabs more than almost any other people seem to arouse the most violent of passions.

The sole purpose of this book is to remedy—in part—this state of ignorance by providing a dose of accurate information, drawn from what I believe to be the best sources, in a form that is at once dense and concise—so concise as to be perhaps too dry for some readers. Its title might have been "Introduction to the Arabs." I aimed for brevity (originally the book was to appear in a pamphlet series, but I could not bring myself to omit certain facts and arguments that I considered essential).

It was obviously impossible to treat everything or even to deal with all the fundamental issues. My "introduction" has therefore focused on a few specific areas. These have been chosen, I trust, to provide a reasonably good likeness of the Arab world, but, more than that, to serve as an aid to understanding the past and to identifying, if nothing else, a few major features already looming on tomorrow's horizon. In short, our goal is to understand the Arabs.

I have chosen not to recount a series of events, nor even to describe the structural evolution of a society in chronological sequence. Nor have I included detailed commentary on individual works and key ideas. Worthy books already exist that treat these topics reasonably well. My first goal has been to define the Arab ethnos [for an explanation of this term, see p. 45 below—trans.], which proved far less easy to do than at first seemed to be the case. In other words, my aim has been to set forth sociological criteria, based on historical data, on the basis of which we might answer the questions: What is an Arab? Who are the Arabs?

At the same time, I have tried to define the present geographical boundaries of the Arab ethnos and explain how they came to be historically. As mentioned above, my purpose in exploring the past is neither to narrate the outstanding events in Arab history nor to describe the social and economic structures underlying that history, but rather to show how each region within the Arab world acquired its Arabhood, and on what ethnic foundations that Arabhood was built. These are issues that have been influential throughout history and continue to be influential today, and yet have been largely ignored, often being concealed from the Arabs themselves by nationalist myths and misunderstood even by specialists in Islamic or Arabic studies—frequently because of their specialization.

After dealing with these questions, it seemed important next to trace in broad outline the story of how Arabism grew out of Arabhood. To put it another way, my goal was to describe and to explain the conditions under which an ideology of ethnic identity—the kind of ideology popularized by modern nationalism—has emerged in this part of the world over the past century or so in forms so complex, contradictory, and, oftentimes, virulent as to surprise and bewilder people in other parts of the world.

My portrait would have been incomplete had I not tried to give some idea—highly schematic, to be sure—of the resources currently and potentially within the grasp of the Arabs, whose ambition is to assume a place—as a free and, as far as possible, a united people—among the most important social groups in the world today.

At this point, what remained to be done was perhaps the most important thing: to characterize the Arabs, to describe them, to sketch their portrait as a group. This was also the most difficult part of my task. Most who have tried their hand at this risky venture before me have succumbed to the temptation to proceed straightaway to a comprehensive portrait tailored in such a way as to make unambiguous judgment possible. Such an end is not easily achieved, or so I believe—at least not if one's purpose is to make no assertions in the absence of well-founded and verifiable evidence, the hallmark of the scientific method. Only with extreme prudence and caution may one venture onto this ground, and even then the rule must be one step at a time—large problems must be broken down into smaller ones until they become tractable. A people is made up of individuals, whose reactions, individually and collectively, are conditioned by the practical and intellectual structures and priorities that inform their actions. I have tried to define—again in a highly concise way—what I take to be the important structures of social relations and of thought among the Arabs. These structures, together with those shared by all mankind, must enter into any attempt to characterize this people, to describe the overall structure of their behavior—what is sometimes called a national character or, in modern terms, a basic personality. In all honesty, I do not believe that this comprehensive structure can be elucidated in detail at present (not even for a subgroup of the Arab people, let alone for all of them), for apart from a few scattered scientific results we have nothing to go on but shrewd guesses. With the help of several other authors, whose insights I have borrowed, I have therefore recorded what I regard as plausible speculation in this regard—no more.

Demythification is my basic concern: the unvarnished facts are my weapons in a war against hackneyed notions that seem to me suspect or false. In this area such notions abound. I have striven for impartiality and tried to reject conclusions urged by nothing more than sentiment tinged to one degree or another by mysticism—though nowadays it is fashionable to make a parade of one's likes and dislikes. While complete objectivity is impossible, still it makes sense to work toward conclusions that have some claim to general validity, rather than to opt deliberately for partiality, like Gribouille, who dove into the water to keep out of the rain. In my view it is no less essential and no less practicable now than ever to employ the tried and true methods of science, relying on verifiable facts (whatever may be said on the matter, there *are* facts independent of our psyches) and observing the rules of rational discourse. The best proof of this assertion is that those who deny its validity invariably try to persuade others to rally to their cause by invoking what they hold to be proven facts and insisting on the selfsame rules of discourse.

Taking such a stand lays one open, of course, to the criticism of those either unable or unwilling to overcome their likes and dislikes, as well as to the charge that scientific dispassion is being used hypocritically to mask one's own sympathies. No argument can convince those who level such accusations.

That remarks such as these are useful if not absolutely necessary may at first sight seem surprising. In a book concerned with the Spanish, the English, or the Chinese, they would be far less necessary. That we must make them is by itself sufficient to make clear the passions aroused today by the question of the Arabs. These passions are also responsible for the many myths that surround our subject, against which we must do battle. Among non-Arabs these myths often reveal rank biogtry; but myths, it should be noted, are also prevalent among the Arabs themselves, where they naturally take on an apologetic cast. Apology inevitably goes hand in hand with distortion and concealment of certain facts. Like non-Arabs who believe fervently in the conventional wisdom, Arabs themselves will find in these pages assertions that contradict what they have been taught. I can do no more than assure them that I have done my utmost to see that nothing is stated here that is not the result of impartial scientific research.

This book is plainly not the work of an Arab, and doubtless this circumstance will be stressed more than it warrants by Arabs who may disagree with me on certain points. Just one more foreigner, they will say, come to scrutinize us, with his prejudices,

his lack of understanding, his culpable malevo-
lence, and his paternalistic benevolence. It is quite
true that, despite my studies and my personal con-
tacts, my foreign origin does prevent my seeing
certain facts or accepting certain points of view; try
as I will, I cannot entirely escape my cultural con-
ditioning as a European. I do not deny this. But it
must also be allowed that the outside observer has
certain advantages. Historians of astronomy tell us
that it has been far more difficult to understand the
structure of our own galaxy, which includes the
entire solar system, than it has been to understand
similar galaxies upon which we gaze from without.
No single point of view is without its advantages
and its disadvantages.

The honest objectivity I am striving to achieve
implies no lack of sympathy for the Arab people,
but my sympathy is not exclusive (why would it be?)
and I try not to be either partial or blind. For
nearly half a century I have followed the ups and
downs of this people and its history, and have kept
up continuous contact with many Arabs after a
rather lengthy residence in their midst. Often I
have seen them unjustly scorned, and still more
often misunderstood. This experience encouraged
me to try to understand them and to make them
understood. To put it another way, I have tried to
attack the myths that have damaged the reputation
of the Arabs among other peoples.

Understanding, however, implies neither indulgence nor servility, neither total love nor willful
blindness, nor does it mean ill will or denigration.
Every people has its heroes and its scoundrels, its

wise men and its fools; all have contributed to mankind's common treasure, and all have collectively made mistakes and errors, and committed crimes. To impassioned supporters and implacable enemies I happily leave such moral comfort as they may derive from their posturing. They clearly have the merit of that holy simplicity that John Hus admired at the stake where he was burned.

⤜ 1 ⤛
Who Are the Arabs?

At first sight, this question seems to admit a simple answer. The Arabs are a people (in anthropological jargon called an "ethnos," while others may say a "nation") well known for their important role in history, spread over a geographical domain stretching from Morocco to Mesopotamia; originally sprung from the cradle of Arabia, they are a people to which this particular name has long been attached both by themselves and by others, and who, finally, speak Arabic, one of the Semitic group of languages. If the Arabs are regarded as forming a nation, it is not a nation-state such as are found in western Europe. The speakers of Arabic, the Arabs, are citizens of several states, only one of which bears the name Arabia, but to which is attached a modifier (Saudi) which limits it scope. According to one terminological convention, therefore, it would be better to regard the Arabs as forming a "nationality" rather than a nation. A powerful movement among the Arabs, however, aims at establishing an Arab nation-state along European lines and claims that to do so would merely be to restore a unity that once existed.

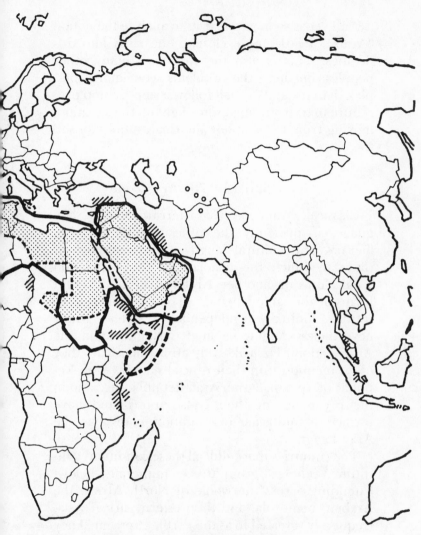

///// Diaspora or major Arab fringe area
━━━━ Boundary of the Arab zone (Arab states)
----- Boundary of the Arab ethnos
━ ━ ━ Boundary of the League of Arab States
°°° Isolated Arab communities

And yet as soon as one tries to analyze the notion "Arabs" a little more closely, one runs into difficulties. This is also the case with many other peoples, but here the problems seem more complex than usual. We shall follow a step-by-step procedure in trying to shed some light on the situation, moving from the simplest and clearest questions to the more complex.

First Approach: The Arab Zone

Classical Arabic, a characteristic Semitic language, is presently the official, administrative, literary, and cultural language of a number of states in which the majority of the population speaks one or another Arabic dialect, different forms of the same language. These countries constitute mutually independent states which nevertheless claim to belong to a single nation, the Arab nation. To make this affiliation clear, they often mention it in their official names (Arab Republic of Yemen, Syrian Arab Republic, etc.) and in the preambles of their constitutions, and have formed a multistate organization known as the Arab League.

The countries that fulfill all these conditions constitute a coherent group (to be enumerated below) extending across the whole of North Africa, the Arabian peninsula, and the western part of Asia, frequently referred to as the Fertile Crescent. They incorporate some 150 million citizens (including some 118 million Arabs, out of a world total of 124 million in 1976) and cover an area of about 13 million square kilometers. This entire region may be called the Arab zone. It is bounded by the Mediterranean, the Turkish and Iranian zones, the Indian Ocean, the Ethiopian region and its outskirts, the countries of black Africa, and the Atlantic.

The Criteria

Language

In most cases the most visible criterion of an ethnos (or people) is language. As mentioned above, Arabic is an independent language within the Semitic language group (along with Akkadian, Hebrew, and the other so-called Canaanite languages, Aramaic and Syriac, the South Arabian dialects, and the Semitic languages of Ethiopia). This group is itself one of the constituents (along with the Berber dialects and ancient Libyan, ancient Egyptian and its Coptic successor, the Kushitic languages of the Ethiopian region, and perhaps some others) of the Hamito-Semitic family of languages.

If it is easy to delimit present-day Arabic in relation to its kindred languages, it is less easy to define it in the remote past. Dispersed throughout the Arabian peninsula are ancient inscriptions (generally quite laconic graffiti) which apparently represent ancient forms of the language. Like most Semitic languages, they are written in a script consisting solely of consonants (not the script of classical or modern Arabic), which leaves us in the dark concerning the finer points of the language or languages. These texts (known as Thamūdic, Ṣafāitic, and Liḥyanite) can nevertheless be linked with Arabic. They have been regarded as constituting a "proto-Arabic" language. This, however, was distinct from the Arabic familiar to us. The most striking difference among those we have been able to discover is that the definite article in proto-Arabic is indicated by the letter *h* (probably read as *ha-*) preceding the noun—as in the Canaanite languages—whereas it appears as *'al-* in all other varieties of Arabic.

Thus the people known as Arabs are normally set apart by the Arabic language. But the criterion is not absolute. As we shall see, the term was long applied by the Arabs themselves only to those who (actually or fictitiously) were connected with one of the tribes inhabiting the Arabian peninsula or its immediate vicinity prior to the Islamic expansion. There were nevertheless increasing numbers of people who spoke Arabic—Arabized people from a linguistic point of view—who were unable to claim such origin, and who for a long period of time were not considered, and did not consider themselves, Arabs. Today, the ideology of Arabism has laid down language as a universally valid criterion—with some exceptions as we shall see (particularly in the case of the Maltese, p. 80).

Culture and History

A famous definition of Arabhood has been given by the eminent British historian of the Arabs and of Islam, H. A. R. Gibb: "All those are Arabs," he wrote, "for whom the central fact of history is the mission of Muḥammad and the memory of the Arab Empire and who in addition cherish the Arabic tongue and its cultural heritage as their common possession."[1]

This definition has some validity. But it gives rise to a number of difficulties. It refuses to bestow Arabhood upon those who in our own time have been convinced that they are Arabs by the success of Arabist ideology, but who have no connection with Islam, such as, to begin with, the many Egyptian and Lebanese Christians. Some refuse to accept an Arab identity even though Arabic is their mother tongue, as is now the case with many Arabic-speaking Jews. Others, who deem themselves Arabs, consider Muḥammad's mission to have been a central fact of history even though they are Christians, since that mission laid the foundations of Arab nationality; they cherish the Arabic tongue along with the cultural heritage it conveys. Still, without renouncing these values there are many who find it possible to look upon the preaching, the death, and the resurrection of Christ as more important than the activities and the teachings of Muḥammad.

Most important, this conception of Arabhood has the disadvantage of cutting all the ties between post-Islamic and pre-Islamic Arabhood. Before Muḥammad the Arab people existed; the Arabs were pagans, Christians, and even Zoroastrians, Jews, or Judaizers. Muḥammad thought of himself as a prophet sent especially to the Arabs and so

1. H. A. R. Gibb, *The Arabs* (Oxford: Clarendon Press, 1940), p. 3 (= *Oxford Pamphlets on World Affairs,* no. 40).

referred to a people already constituted before his advent. At the very least, then, we need to complete Gibb's definition by giving another applicable to the pre-Islamic Arabs.

Then, too, all non-Arab Muslims (who probably account for nearly four-fifths of the Muslim community) hold as a matter of principle that Muḥammad's mission was the central fact of history. Most of them revere, even if they do not know, the Arabic tongue as the language of the Revelation and, in a word, as the language of God. Literate believers use the language and cherish its literature. A typical instance is Pakistan, a state that regards itself as based on Muslim religion and even considered the possibility of adopting Arabic as an official language. Still, there are many Persians, Turks, Malays, Indonesians, etc., who do not consider themselves, and are not considered, Arabs (some exceptions to this rule will be mentioned later on).

In speaking of a cherished cultural heritage, Gibb, striking an elitist note, is thinking solely of the high culture of learning and art. But the phenomena in question involved millions of men, here as elsewhere mostly illiterate until recent times. It is far preferable, therefore, to consider culture in the sense in which the term is used by anthropologists. Culture consists of the whole range of behavior that is learned and transmitted socially, along with all the works that make it manifest: technical activities (including medical techniques), economic, cognitive, and artistic practices (including the humblest and most ephemeral expressions of the aesthetic impulse), juridical practices in the broadest possible sense of the term (modes of grouping, kinship relations, etc.), ideological practices (meaning essentially religion in premodern societies), etc. History is also a cultural phenomenon in the sense that what is important in ensuring the cohesiveness of a people or of any grouping is less the objective reality of a series of events than the socially elaborated and transmitted image of those events as conceived by the group.

From the cultural point of view, as far as the Arabs are concerned, we have to be explicit about periods and locales. To begin with, there is the core of the present people, the Arabs of Arabia—the only Arabs before Islam, and even then Arabs were widely scattered over outlying regions, where they had not been completely assimilated by the neighboring populations. These Arabian Arabs—to be distinguished as we shall see, from the pre-Islamic South Arabians—had (and in large part still do have) a common culture, a distinctive set of social behaviors that sets them apart from neighboring peoples. These neighbors did not fail to observe and record these differences. Thus there was an Arab cultural unity which has been more or less preserved in Arabia.

The great Arab conquests of the seventh and eight centuries dispersed a considerable portion of the Arabian tribes over a vast area stretching from the Indus to the Pyrenees. During this period the Arabs ruled an enormous empire inhabited by a variety of peoples: Romanized Iberians and Goths in Spain, Berbers, Egyptians, Syrians, Mesopotomians, Iranians, etc. A segment of these tribes kept to the pastoral way of life they had known in the

Arabian peninsula, and as a consequence preserved much of the original culture. Others abandoned this way of life and adopted many of the
cultural traits characteristic of the peoples among
whom they were living, and with whom they
merged. These peoples themselves were largely assimilated to the Arabian Arabs and became
Arabized, adopting (frequently, at any rate) the
language, the new religion, and some of the traditions of the Arabs. It should be borne in mind, as
always, that some of them converted to Islam without adopting the Arabic language (like the Iranians
and later the Turks), while others adopted the
Arabic tongue without converting to Islam (as was
the case with some Christians and Jews, in numbers
that diminished steadily with time).

The result of this slow process of partial fusion,
the extent of which varied from region to region, is
the present-day Arab people, composed largely of
fairly recently Arabized elements, though in many
cases they believe themselves to be descendants of
Arabian Arabs. But the culture of the originally
non-Arab peoples has in large part subsisted, expressed in Arabic and frequently graced with the
sanctifying mantle of Islam, with which Arabian
Arab traditions have mingled. It is easy to uncover
remnants of ancient Egyptian behavioral patterns
in today's Arabized Egypt, as well as Aramaic elements in the present-day Arab culture of the Fertile Crescent.

It is therefore apparent that one must abandon
the widely held notion according to which an Arab
civilization or culture formed in Arabia is supposed

to have spread in the wake of the conquests over a vast expanse of the planet, unchanged or at most slightly modified and supplemented by local accretions. The reality was far more complex. The civilization of the Arabized countries is only in part a continuation of pre-Islamic Arab culture. Ever since the early Middle Ages this civilization has embodied a new synthesis in which the legacy of the ancient cultures of the Near East, combined, assimilated, and to some extent altered by events occuring in the time of the ancient empires and later during a thousand years of Hellenization, has played a large part.

A culture can be analyzed in terms of cultural features whose territorial extent varies. The everyday, practical, popular culture of the contemporary Arab world exhibits a variety of features, many of which extend over only a portion of the Arab zone and in some cases outside it. Diet, for instance, differs from one Arab region to the next, a fact that may surprise many Frenchmen, who know a bit about the Maghrib and therefore believe that Arabs in the East feast on couscous and mint tea. While family life is largely the same over the entire area, similar behavior is found in non-Arab Muslim areas.

By contrast, high culture, the culture of the elite, does exhibit a greater degree of unity, and here Gibb's definition regains some of its value. The members of the elite are all communicants in a single cult of Arab history, Arab literature (including that of its early pre-Islamic period, the work of the Arabian Arabs), and the classical

Arabic tongue. This attachment to an intellectual culture associated with Islamic traditions, which sanctify even its originally non-Muslim aspects, has been a very potent unifying influence. Furthermore, this influence has extended even to the masses owing to the prestige attaching to the elite in a hierarchical society in which everything associated with Islam acquires a sacred ideological character.

Arab Awareness

The most important criterion is probably awareness of Arab identity. To say this is by no means to reduce the national or ethnic phenomenon to a question of psychology. Ethnic awareness is not breathed in from the atmosphere, but rather grows out of specific situations. The emergence of an awareness of ethnic or national identity, however, is a significant historical development in its own right, through which the forces pregnant in the situation make themselves felt.

The problem, however, is not a simple one. To begin with, what is the nature of this awareness? There are distinctions to be made. Some people possess an awareness of being Arabs (or some other nationality) even though not all members of their own group and not all outsiders would concur (this is the case with a good many Christians, especially in the past, as well as with certain Jews today, as far as one segment of Muslim Arab opinion is concerned). By contrast, there are others who consider themselves to be non-Arabs but who are regarded by outsiders (particularly by Arab nationalists) as Arabs (this is the case with many Berbers and

Kurds, for example). Other cases are even more complex. The judgment of a particular individual or group as to his or its own situation, or the situation of others, may vary from time to time. Instances of this are not unknown in countries that may be more familiar to the reader: in France, for instance, many Bretons, Basques, Occitans, and Corsicans, who used to consider themselves French, descendants of families that used to take fierce pride in belonging to the French nation, have in recent years abruptly discovered new identities, gone on to organize regionalist movements, and even been heard to shout the slogan "French go home!" To move beyond this fundamental question, we must also take note of the fact that men perceive and assert their identity in different ways. What is more, these ways develop through several stages. The evidence needed to follow this evolution with any degree of confidence is unfortunately lacking.

Did the tribes of ancient Arabia that spoke Arabic or proto-Arabic see themselves as having a common identity? Did they call themselves "Arabs"? All we are certain of is that early in the first millennium B.C. their neighbors to the north applied this term to a group of tribes in the northern portion of the Arabian peninsula. In Akkadian the name was Aribi, Arabi, Arubu, Urbu; in Hebrew it was 'Arab. It made its earliest appearance in a text of the Assyrian king Shalmaneser III. In 853 B.C. at Qarqar in Syria he defeated a coalition of Syrian and Israelite kings with 1000 cameleers "from Gindibu in the Arabi country."

The etymology of the word is obscure, as is the case with the names of many peoples. The most attractive hypothesis links it to a Semitic name for the steppe, 'Arabah, which among other things denotes the low-lying area that stretches southward from the Dead Sea. The meaning of the word is supposed to have broadened gradually (cf. Germany, Palestine). Another candidate sometimes mentioned is a Semitic root connoting "confused mixture." The supposition is that the nomads proudly adopted a disparaging term applied to them by others, a word that contrasted their way of life with the organized but servile life of the sedentary tribes.[2]

Perhaps the Greeks, in the wake of the Persians,[3] extended this term to apply to the whole peninsula. For Herodotus (3:107) Arabia was the last of the inhabited lands of the southern coast. All its inhabitants were Arabs.

The South Arabians, however, did not regard themselves as Arabs. They were farmers and city-dwellers who had established well-run states endowed with complex structures and highly developed techniques; for them, the word "Arabs" applied exclusively to the nomadic shepherds of the northern and central portions of the peninsula, who spoke Arabic or proto-Arabic. They themselves spoke a similar, but not identical, Semitic language. At most they may have acknowledged a

2. Martin Hartmann, *Der islamische Orient: II. Die Arabische Frage* (Leipzig: R. Haupt, 1909), pp. 113 ff.

3. Concerning the extent of the *Arabāya* of the Persians, see F.-M. Abel, *Géographie de la Palestine* (Paris: Gabalda, 1938), vol. 2, pp. 113 ff.

distant kinship with these "savage" Arabs, of whom they were by and large contemptuous.

Present opinion favors the hypothesis that the groups that spoke Arabic and the South Arabian dialects migrated from the north during the second millennium. They slowly assimilated their predecessors in the region, of whom Arab legends preserve traces. Very widely dispersed, these clans have left behind no more than a few stone tools and perhaps a few cave drawings and place-names. Before the camel the ass was the common means of transportation.

The earliest inscription in true Arabic is found on the tombstone of Nemara on the fringe of the Syrian desert. King Imru'ul-Qays, who died in A.D. 328, there declares himself "king of all the Arabs." But we do not know precisely what he meant by this.

Not until the sixth century A.D. do we come into possession of abundant indigenous documentation, in the form of pre-Islamic poetry in Arabic. Virtually no use is made in this material of the word "Arab." But the term was known. Derivative forms attest to the fact. It was used to contrast tribes sharing the same culture and language with other ethnic elements.[4]

Already tribal genealogists were confidently constructing family trees for these segmentary Semitic-speaking societies. Exhibiting great variety,

---

4. This was proven, against the contentions of D. H. Müller, by the great orientalist Theodor Nöldeke in his invaluable article, "Arabia," in *Encyclopedia Biblica, A Critical Dictionary* (London: Black, 1899), vol. 1, col. 272–75. See also the article cited in the following note.

these artificial systems often expressed the alliance of two tribes, for instance, by setting their eponymous ancestors down as brothers. Such systematic genealogies encompassing all the Arab tribes have not come down to us from any earlier than just before the advent of Islam. In at least one of them we find the assertion that the original inhabitants of Arabia—referred to as "the vanished Arabs" (*al-'Arab al-bā'ida*) or even "the real Arabs" (*al -'Arab al-'āriba*)—had all vanished well before the inception of Islam.

Later, all the Arabian tribes, including those of South Arabia, by that time fully Arabized, were tied in to the genealogy found in chapter 10 of Genesis. There it is said that they were divided into two branches. The ancestor of the northern and central tribes, we are told, was 'Adnān, descendant of Ishmael, son of Abraham. Paradoxically, these are supposed to have been "Arabized Arabs" (*muta 'arriba* or *musta 'riba*), whereas the appellation "real Arabs' (*al-'āriba or al-'arbā'*) was given to the South Arabians, who were supposed to be children of one Qaḥtān, identified with the biblical Yoqtān, a direct descendant of Shem, son of Noah. This classification reflects the struggles for prestige and power of the first centuries of Islam. Based on what we know today, we would argue for the opposite point of view. But many variants of these genealogies are known.

In one of its connotations, the word "Arab" has always referred to a way of life. Essentially, it denotes an Arabic-speaking nomadic shepherd, a Bedouin. The only form of the word attested by the

Koran (apart from the designation of the language) is *al-A'rāb,* a doublet of the general ethnographic term (*al-'Arab*), which specifically designated the Bedouins.

Thus in the time of the Prophet, the Arabic-speaking tribes had a vague ethnic awareness based on language and on shared cultural traits. In all likelihood, the South Arabians were acknowledged to have a particularly close relationship with this "Arab" group, which was contrasted as a whole with the "foreigners" (*al-'Ajam*). This moral tie was reinforced by the great fairs, the literary and oratorical contests between tribes, the sanctuaries to which many people made pilgrimages, and other intertribal institutions (sacred truces, calendar, etc.).[5]

From 613 (approximately) to 632, Muḥammad and his propagandists increasingly appealed to national feeling to rally the Arabs to the new doctrine, which was universally valid but preached in a specific form intended especially for them. In the ninth year of the Hegira (630–31) Muḥammad's official poet invited a delegation from the Tamīm tribe to accept Islam by uttering these verses (among others):

"Compare no other to God, become Muslims! Do not dress any longer as foreigners do!"[6]

The conquests carried out by the Prophet's suc-

5. Cf. G. E. von Grunebaum, "The Nature of Arab Unity before Islam," *Arabica* 10 (1963):4–23.

6. Ibn Hishām, *Sīra,* ed. F. Wüstenfeld, (Göttingen, 1859–60), p. 938; trans. A. Guillaume, *The Life of Muhammad* (London, 1955), pp. 630–31.

cessors established an immense empire in which
the ruling caste was Arab and determined to hold
on to its power. The distinctive feature of this caste
was that it was Muslim. Among the masses of subject peoples, Christians, Jews, and some others
were allowed to keep their religion in return for
payment of a special tax. This was justified in light
of their monotheism, a doctrine that was held to be
substantially correct, even if Islam had transcended
their dogmas and shown their sacred books to be
partly false. The Arabs, however, were obliged to
be Muslims.

Under the Umayyads (660–750), who ruled this
Arab empire, it was possible to join the ruling caste
by adopting Islam and entering into a client relationship with an Arab tribe—in other words, by
undergoing Arabization. So as not to swell exces-
sively the ranks of the ruling caste, restrictions were
placed on conversion, which obviously had the effect of reducing its total revenue and limiting the
share of each member.

These restrictions could not be maintained in-
definitely, however. If Islam was the truth as re-
vealed by God, it seemed scandalous to deprive
anyone of it. The Arabs were only the agents by
which the truth was spread.

Islamization thus continued without always
leading to Arabization. Some Persians, Turks, and
Berbers became Muslims without joining the
Arabs, and they continued to speak their own languages, even though Arabic was the liturgical, intellectual, and scientific language used when necessary by their scholars, particularly in their writings.

Under the Abbasid Empire (after 750) the Arabs lost their most important privileges. This was a state that was Muslim but no longer Arab. Heterogeneous Muslim ethnic groups coexisted within this empire and in the states to which its disintegration gave rise: Arabs, Turks, Persians, Berbers, etc.

From this point on, the distinction became more and more marked between the group of Arabic-speakers as a whole and those who may be regarded as belonging to the Arab ethnos. Gradually, the terminology came to reflect this difference. Increasingly, the tendency was to reserve the term 'Arab exclusively for the Bedouins, associated (historically, at least, and often wrongly) with the nomadic way of life practiced in ancient Arabia: the descendants of the Arab ruling caste of the Umayyad Empire together with the "clients" who had affiliated themselves with the ancient tribes—people who could remember no other origin (or of whom others could remember no other origin), all of them Muslims. As for the bulk of the settled urban and rural population, which incorporated many people who spoke other languages and did not claim to have been affiliated with the Arabian tribes, the term that soon gained currency was *awlād al-'Arab* (or *abnā' al-'Arab*), "the children, the descendants of the Arabs."[7]

A primary or secondary criterion of Arabhood in this sense was (probably after some hesitation on

7. The meaning of the expression has changed as circumstances dictated and is frequently used today in the East to mean simply Arabs in the modern sense of the word, i.e., speakers of Arabic.

this score) the Muslim religion. The Egyptian
Christians among whom the Coptic language
gradually gave way to Arabic, the Christian peasants of the Fertile Crescent who likewise turned
slowly from Aramaic to Arabic, and the Jews who
customarily spoke Arabic were not in general included under the concept of Arabs or "children of
Arabs." Even if they converted to Islam, frequently
retaining thereafter some degree of cohesiveness
and distinctiveness for long periods of time, words
indicative of their past associations were frequently
applied to them.[8]

Ethnic rivalries emerged within this highly composite society. They are known to us almost exclusively through literature. There is a considerable
body of writing praising the merits and listing the
faults of one group or another. Frequently these
are rival cliques fighting over the monopoly of a
particular category of administrative posts. In the
Abbasid era there was a whole literary movement,
mainly Persian, in which the party known as the
shu'ūbīya attacked the preeminence of the Arabs.
Other writers answered the charges. But the merits
and defects attributed to the Arabs always applied
to the Arabian Arabs, people connected with the
peninsular tribes. The *awlād al-'Arab* do not come
under scrutiny. Furthermore, many of the anti-
Arabs were Arabized Iranians who were sometimes
described as *muta'arriba*, extending a term formerly
limited to tribes supposed to be descended from

8. See especially A. N. Poliak, "L'arabisation de l'Orient sémitique,"
Revue des études islamiques, 1938, pp. 35–63.

'Adnān.[9] The ethnos that was aware of its Arab-hood and regarded as Arab by others, that was under attack by a broadly based social movement represented by the writers, was therefore not identified by use of Arabic. By the same token, the Persians and the Turks, who regarded themselves, and were regarded, as such, included a large proportion of Arabized elements.

In any case, we do not yet find, and will not find for some time to come, the modern idea of a national state in which the rulers must share the ethnic origins of the ruled. Following the tradition inherited from the Christian Roman Empire, the unity of the state was based on the religious ideology of the ruling caste. Political allegiance went either to the state, the dynasty, or to the various local groups, such as tribes, villages, cities and districts, and religious communities.

These circumstances are basically responsible for the lack of interest throughout this period in the notion of belonging to an ethnic group and in the specific terms connoting such belonging. City-dwellers were in general called *al-ḥaḍar,* meaning settled in the strict sense, regardless of their language and origins. The *'Arab* were nomads whose natural habitat was the desert, as well as those who continued to observe the customs of the nomadic way of life. The great sociologist and historian Ibn Khaldūn (1332–1406), who was born in Tunis to a family that hailed originally from Arabia and that

9. Cf. G. Lecomte, *Ibn Qutayba*, (Damascus: Institut français, 1965), p. 348.

had invaded Spain with the conquerors, hence, according to the modern conception, a true Arab,
does indeed speak frequently of the Arabs as this
conquering people, but in general contemptuously
identifies the Arabs with the uncultured nomads,
still at the tribal level of existence and by nature
destructive. This was the basis for his celebrated
play on words concerning the countries conquered
by the Arabs (al-'Arab), which were promptly
turned into wastelands (al-kharāb).[10]

The extension of the term to all speakers of
Arabic came about only very gradually. In all
likelihood it took place first in the regions in which
they were foreigners. Thus at Istanbul in the sixteenth century, a small number of Egyptians, Syrians, and Iraqis who worked in construction or at
ceramics and were largely confined to one quarter
of town had a special mosque known as 'Arab jāmi 'i,
"the mosque of the Arabs."[11]

Decisive changes began to occur only in the
eighteenth century. From the sixteenth century on,
virtually the whole of the region in which Arabic
was spoken was ruled by the Ottoman Empire. Like
the Near Eastern states that preceded it, it was
based not on nationality but on religion. It was a
Muslim state in which theoretically all Muslims of
free status were equals as first-class subjects. The
sultans were Turks, but they ruled through slaves

10. Ibn Khaldūn, *Muqaddima*, ed. Quatremère, 1, p. 270; ed. Wafi,
(Cairo, 1957–62), 2, p. 453; trans. F. Rosenthal, (New York, 1958), 1,
p. 302; trans. V. Monteil (Beirut, 1967–68), 1, p. 295.

11. R. Mantran, *Istanbul dans la seconde moitié du XVIIe siècle,* (Paris:
Adrien-Maisonneuve, 1962), p. 64.

of different origins. In the eighteenth century the
state was more and more under the thumb of the
free Turks, and the subjects, whether Muslim or
not, felt that the Turks ruled them. The sharp decline in the degree of control over the provinces
exercised by the central authorities afforded relatively great powers to the local elites in each region,
particularly to the *'ulamā'*, the men of religion, and
to a partially overlapping, associated group, the
ashrāf, who claimed to be descendants of the
Prophet and who were consequently especially re-
vered. All prided themselves on their Arab origin
and their knowledge of Arabic, and naturally they
took advantage of this in seeking some measure of
autonomy under the Turks. For mass support, they
usually turned to the community of their supposed
ancestors. In the cities, centers of this new type of
power, the descendants of Arab tribes had long
since merged with Arabized elements, and all
Arabic-speaking Muslims considered themselves
Arabs. This went hand in hand with continuing
contempt for and hostility toward the Bedouin
nomads, who were still seen as Arabs and whose
devastating raids increased in ferocity owing to the
weakness of the state. In addition, Christians in the
Arab countries, like the Jews made prosperous by
the expansion of trade, especially with Europe,
abandoned their former languages once and for
all, introduced Arabic even into the liturgy, cultivated themselves with the help of the papacy,
which recruited among them Catholics with
allegiance to Rome, and set up printing shops,
seminaries, and schools. They turned to the study

of Arabic literature and sought out instruction
from Muslim scholars, with whom they entered
into close relations. Increasingly, they felt themselves to be Arabs.[12]

Under these conditions, the revolts and local
movements of centrifugal tendency took on an
anti-Turkish character. This was the case even in
Arabia with Wahhābism, which was basically a
movement of religious reform, but which reflected
centrifugal political tendencies and under the force
of circumstance assumed the form of an Arab state
(1744–1818). When Ibrahīm, son of the Egyptian
pasha Muḥammad ʿAlī, conquered the Arab countries Arabia (1816) and Syria-Palestine (1832–40) in
his father's behalf, the project of creating a great
Arab state took shape in his mind—even though he
was Albanian through and through—as well as in
the minds of various European politicians, particularly in France.[13] The revolt of the Greeks, who
won independence from the Ottoman Empire
(1821–29), served as an example, first of all for the
Christian nationalities of the Empire, but also because of the fillip it gave to the idea of a nation
based on ethno-linguistic association, which gradually won men's minds. Thus during the nineteenth
century, people, and to begin with Christians, grew
accustomed to the idea of an Arab nationality
whose vocation was to acquire at least a modicum of

12. Here I can do no more than summarize the very fine article by
Albert Hourani, "The Changing Face of the Fertile Crescent in the
Eighteenth Century," *Studia Islamica* 8 (1957):89–122.
13. Many details are given in J. Hajjar, *L'Europe et les destinées du
Proche-Orient (1815–1848)*, (Paris: Bloud and Gay, 1970).

political autonomy. Arab awareness achieved a new clarity and increasingly eroded the idea of a religiously based allegiance.

We shall have more to say later on about the contemporary development of the concept of Arabism, or a modern type of nationalism based on Arab self-awareness. For now it will be enough to summarize its complex origins. The criterion of ethnic identity, of belonging to a vast group supposed to share a common origin, characterized by a name and by common cultural features, and above all circumscribed by the bounds of the linguistic community, had a good deal of validity in antiquity and in the early years of the Muslim Empire. An ethno-national ideology helped bind together members of an unorganized ethnos.[14] Closely tied to a universalist religious ideology, Islam, it contributed to the success of the latter and was for a time identified with it. But this religious ideology, having provided mortar to build an empire, and later several multiethnic states, in the end overshadowed—to say the least—and even obliterated this Arab ethno-national ideology. The latter ideology lived on in a state of latency, however, supported by a half-finished foundation: the cultural traits common to the group (based on the Bedouin way of life, which was taken as a norm even by people who were abandoning it) and the glory of a prestigious common history. Belief in Islam, a faith founded in and by the nation, was

14. Concerning these concepts, I refer the reader to my theoretical essay, "Nation et idéologie," in *Encyclopaedia Universalis* (Paris, 1971), vol. 11, pp. 571–75.

included among these common cultural traits. The other customary basis of ethno-national ideology, language, played in the main a negative role, generally being used to deny ethnic identity to groups exhibiting a similar way of life, but not speaking Arabic. By itself it was not enough to legitimate integration into the ethnos of non-Muslims or even Arabized people (and, at times, even genuine Arabs) who simply had too little in common with that particular way of life. To achieve a hegemonic position, an ethno-national ideology based on a language criterion (with exceptions to be mentioned later) and taking as its ideal the creation of nation-state required the following conditions: (1) worldwide ascendancy of ethno-national ideologies with linguistic demarcation; (2) a tendency to secularization; and (3), last but not least, the rise of a multiconfessional Arabic-speaking bourgeoisie with common interests, engaged in a more or less unified struggle.

Mistaken Criteria

Islam

History has known the Arab ethnos for twenty-nine centuries. For fifteen centuries it subscribed to paganism, Judaism, Zoroastorianism, and above all Christianity. Furthermore, out of some of 550 million Muslims (?) in the world today, approximately 150 million are Arabs. More than three-quarters, then, belong to other ethnic groups and speak other languages. This should suffice to put an end to the common error of Westerners in frequently confusing the notions "Arab" and "Muslim." The press has even blamed the Arabs for the behavior of the Indonesians and the Pakistanis!

One thing that helps to perpetuate this confusion is the current vogue for the term "Arab Muslim." If this phrase has any meaning other than to distinguish Muslim from Christian Arabs in, for instance, Lebanon, it can only be to indicate that, historically, *for the Arabs*, the ethno-national factor has been closely related to the religious factor in the determination of what may be called, in Hichem Djaït's words, the "Arabo-Islamic personality."[15]

Having said this, it remains true, as we have seen, that the Arab ethnos does have an especially close relationship with Islam. The Prophet of Islam, who spoke to all men, was an Arab prophet. The Arab ethnos was the core group of the religion and responsible for its spread. The Koran, the word of God, is written in Arabic, so that Muslims on the whole regard Arabic as the language of God. Throughout the Muslim world scholars study Arabic, which is among other things the language of theology. Even many illiterates learn the Koran by heart in Arabic without understanding it. It is in principle forbidden to translate it. Just as Christianity introduced many Greek and Latin words into other languages, so Islam has diffused similar Arabic terms over an immense linguistic zone.

It cannot be taken for granted that the nineteenth- and twentieth-century trend toward

15. Hichem Djaït, *La personnalité et le devenir arabo-islamiques* (Paris: Seuil, 1974).

integration of Arabic-speaking Christians and Jews
of the Near East into the Arab ethnos as full members will continue. Within the Muslim world these
Jewish and Christian communities at one time had
the unique advantage of relatively close ties to
Europe during the era of European domination.
The masses most viscerally opposed to European
hegemony were found among the Muslims. With
that hegemony on the wane in the wake of
nationalist victories in the Third World, Christians
and Jews found that they were compromised by
deep-seated memories of those past ties and their
consequences. In the popular mind, whose feelings
rarely find overt expression on an intellectual or
political level, there is a sense that the true Arab,
the Arab who kept faith with his origins, is first and
foremost the Muslim Arab. In the case of the Jews
the question is already practically closed, for they
frequently opted for the foreign culture, and the
colonizers sometimes encouraged this to win their
allegiance (for example, the Crémieux decree in
Algeria, which in 1870 granted political rights to
Jews, though not to Arabs). The possibility of
forging a link with Arabism, for which the anticolonialist efforts of certain Jews paved the way
(Jacob Sanua for one, who was a comrade of Jamāl
ad-dīn al-Afghānī and Muḥammad ʿAbduh in
Egypt), was foreclosed by Zionism and its successful
attempt to create a Jewish state on Arab territory,
in Palestine, and the consequences thereof.

The earliest pioneers of contemporary Arab
nationalism were recruited among the Christians of
the East. Obviously, it was in their interest to base

the ideology on the linguistic and cultural community at the expense of the religious identification that tied the Muslim Arabs to their Turkish rulers. They did not stint in their proclamations of uncompromising Arabism. They glorified the Prophet of Islam as a hero of Arab nationalism, and in doing so fell in with a deep-seated secularizing tendency among Muslims themselves. The major theoretician of the Ba'th, or lay nationalist party, was Michel 'Aflaq, a Christian.

At present, however, the historical logic of the situation is pointing in another direction. History has so arranged matters that the onset of new crises has not allowed a sufficient time for the secularization process to be completed or for the various confessions to become closely integrated. We have only to recall how long this took in most parts of Europe. For one thing, the clergy is a powerful pressure group, backed by the masses, who remain devoted to a religious ideology that did not betray them and that sanctified their humble ethics and values as against the aristocrats' Europeanizing "debauchery," both intellectual and moral. In most countries in the region this pressure group has been successful in having Islam established as a state religion, or at least as a majority religion, within the national constitutions themselves. Then, too, in Lebanon, where the situation was somewhat similar to that in Israel, a political split developed along the lines of confessional cleavage. One segment of the Lebanese Christian community, primarily Maronite, looked to Europe and particularly to France as a prestigious cultural model,

and to the predominantly Muslim Arab neighbors
as antagonists. Even though this group had provided Arabist ideology with its earliest and
foremost exponents, many of them turned to
France for protection, if need be, against the
mounting tide of Arabism, which was identified
with Islam and with the continuation or restoration
of Muslim dominance. French imperialism was
only too happy to make use of these willing and
ethusiastic satellites. It is true that in Islamo-
Christian Lebanon a compromise was struck between wealthy Christians and Muslims, at first
under the aegis of the French mandate and later in
struggle against it for total independence of the
native elites; for a time there was reason to believe
that a broad tide was running to the Arabist cause.
This tide continued to rise among the propertyless,
the intellectuals, and the left. Nevertheless, the
seeds of intestine struggle had already been
sown, with the parties hewing closely to the lines
of the confessional split, accentuated by the archaic clan structures of the society. Today the battle
has reached fever pitch. No one can say what the
ultimate solution will be. For the moment conflict
has deepened suspicions that elsewhere were on
the wane and has led once again to inclusion of
Islam as one of the distinctive features of Arab nationality.

Arab Civilization or Islamic Civilization?

The brilliant civilization that grew up in the
Middle Ages in the countries that the Arabs conquered but ceased to rule after a century or two is

called by some "Arab" civilization, by others "Muslim" (or "Islamic") civilization, and by still others
"Muslim Arab" civilization. Ideological commit-
ment for and against modern Arab nationalism has
been at least partly responsible for this battle of
nomenclature.

The term "civilization" is a doublet for the term
"culture," with all the usual ambiguity and contradiction attendant upon the use in common parlance of abstract terminology. The rather limited
currency acquired by the more or less precise anthropological meaning connected with the word
"culture" has been enough to encourage a tendency to restrict the use of the word "civilization" to
the most prestigious exemplars of intellectual and
artistic activity. Now, where the "civilization" in
question is concerned, it happens to have been
these intellectual and aesthetic ingredients that
exerted a strong influence on neighboring civiliza-
tions, Christian western Europe in particular,
during the Middle Ages.

During that period the Muslim world exhibited a
great many common cultural traits (in the broadest
possible sense), of which there were numerous
variants. To enter that world from the outside was
to feel that one had ventured into a world different
from one's own, with its own specific character. It
happens that the most common and definite of
these distinctive cultural features belonged to the
intellectual, aesthetic, and moral sphere usually
denoted by the word "civilization."

Central to this special and unique world was religion, at least the politically dominant religion, the

state ideology of Islam. The Muslim countries, despite their cultural differences and political hostilities, and notwithstanding the alliances that some of them were to form with "infidels" against others, constituted what we may call an ideologico-political bloc, the *dār al-Islām*, "the home of Islam." This bloc is roughly comparable with the present-day ideologico-political blocs that group (albeit rather loosely, as has been clear for the past twenty years) countries subscribing to Marxist-communist ideology on the one hand and to liberal capitalist ideology on the other.

The unity of the Muslim bloc was a consequence neither of language nor of ethnicity, factors deemed of no political importance during this period. The great intellectual and aesthetic achievements of this civilization were the work of people who spoke Arabic, Turkish, Persian, Berber, or some other language in daily life. Some referred to themselves as Arabs, Turks, Persians, Berbers, etc., but many considered themselves merely Muslims of mixed origin.

The civilization that they created should therefore be called Islamic (the adjective "Muslim" should properly be reserved for a religious context). However, the intellectual language known to all cultivated men of the period and usually used when they composed works of high intellectual power—as opposed to their mother tongue, which was kept for family use, for poetry, and for letters in general—was Arabic, the language of the Koran, of theology, and of ideological analysis and intellectual discourse. Hence it has been argued that this civilization may be called "Arab," just as we call "Roman" an equally multiethnic civilization in which the dominant language (along with Greek) was Latin, the language of Rome.

There are advantages and disadvantages to both appellations. It is impossible to compress all the elements of a definition into a single word. The term "Islamic civilization" is the more objective even though it fails to indicate that Christians and Jews played an important part in the major creations (and in most aspects of the culture) stemming from the cultural zone dominated by Islam. The term Arab, looked at askance by the Iranians and Turks among others, lays stress on the ethnic origin of the Muslim ideological mortar and on the language that was the favored vehicle of this culture. It is of course preferred by Arabs who suspect conscious or unconscious anti-Arabism on the part of anyone who uses another. But it ill serves the large number of people who played important roles in this culture and this civilization and who considered themselves neither Arabs nor "children of Arabs"—Arabized. The mixed term "Arab Muslim" has the disadvantage of implying an equivalence between its two components. It can be applied with full justice only to Muslims claiming Arab origins.

The disadvantages emerge clearly when one takes up the problem of the petrification or decadence of this civilization. The Arabs describe as "decadent" (*inḥiṭāṭ*) the entire period during which supremacy in the Islamic world passed into the hands of states ruled by Turks (or under Turkish

influence), particularly when these states dominated the Arab-speaking areas. But the sixteenth
and seventeenth centuries, a decadent period for
the subject Arabs, belong to an era during which
Islam under Ottoman Turk leadership won daz-
zling victories, and during which the Ottoman, Iranian, and Indian Mughal empires attained a high
cultural brilliance graced by magnificent artistic
and intellectual creations.

One form of anti-Arab polemic, striking a racist
note, has tried to capitalize on the multiethnic
character of the medieval civilization to deny that
Arabs possess any powers of cultural creativity or
"civilized" qualities. The exponents of this view are
unwittingly rehearsing the arguments of the
medieval *shu'ūbiya.* This line of reasoning exhibits
an obnoxious conceptual confusion and no small
measure of bigoted bad faith. The creative in-
tellects within this civilization were either Arabs,
Arabized, or Muslims not to be regarded in any
sense as Arabs. If the number of genuine Arabs
descended from the tribes of the Arabian peninsula and belonging to this elite was relatively
small, this was merely because the total number of
genuine Arabs was small compared to the number
of Arabized people, and perforce to the total
number of Muslims. But among the creators were a
great many Arabized people. Now today, the
Arabized elements are in the majority among those
who call themselves, and who are rightly called,
Arabs. It is therefore inconsistent and disingenu-
ous to deny that present-day Arabs have cultural
qualities by pointing to the small number of Ara-

bian Arabs among the creative individuals of another epoch.[16] Such attacks may explain why the Arabs are attached to the term "Arab civilization" to describe the Islamic civilization of the Middle Ages, though since we aim to be objective, we may accept it only with reservations.

Race

Even today it is not uncommon to hear people speak of the "Arab race," and "that filthy race" is an insult that comes easily to the lips of racist ex-colonists of the Maghrib. Despite the many attempts to demystify the idea of race that accompanied the fight against the Nazis and continued after their defeat, there is still need for elementary clarification of the confused concepts associated with this notion.

In the human species we do not find sharply defined groups the characteristics of whose offspring we can predict with certainty, as is the case with the various breeds [*races* in French—trans.] of dogs. There are, however, certain basic groups, relatively distinctive from a genetic point of view, whose members are more likely to mate with one another than with members of other groups, and hence, in accordance with Mendel's laws, transmit a significant number of physical characteristics to subsequent generations. Significantly, however, these reproductive units are never wholly hermetic,

16. I developed this line of thought at somewhat greater length in my 1961 article, "Maghreb et nationalisme arabe," reprinted with a new introduction in my book, *Marxisme et monde musulman* (Paris: Seuil, 1972), pp. 527–54.

and under the conditions prevailing at present
tend to be less and less so. They are ambiguous
groups of fluctuating composition whose boundaries are imprecisely defined, homogeneous only in
a statistical sense.

The trend has been to drop the term "race" as a
designation for such groups. The hope is thus to
avoid such unfortunate consequences as the
identification of these groups with animal breeds,
the carry-over into scientific ideologies of mistaken
notions connected with the term, and the ter-
minologically engendered confusion between these
classes and the typological classifications of human
groups that have become traditional over the past
century of two. These typologies have been based
mainly on common visible characters, to which
were linked (despite continual warnings from the
physical anthropologists) purely cultural traits.
Now, if these physical characters are in fact hereditary, the modalities of their transmission are not
well understood, owing to the complexity of their
relation to specific genes. It is now clear that the
characters that should be looked at are nonap-
parent characters, which are manifestly connected
with gene structure, impervious to cultural and en-
vironmental influences, and readily classifiable. A
suitable choice has proved to be the so-called blood
markers, which can be studied through analysis of
the blood.

As a term for denoting the primary reproductive
units, "populations" is therefore preferable. This
word may also be a poor choice, however, because
its ambiguity in common parlance would seem to

leave no room for the idea of a set of hereditary somatic characters that are common, in at least a statistical sense, to a particular group.

The present state of the art, then, permits characterization of small subgroups of the human species, of which all told there are no doubt a great many. It is quite difficult to determine the relations among these various "populations," each of which is the temporary product of innumerable matings. The various characteristics of any one group are not perfectly correlated with the other characteristics of the same group, since essentially each character has a distribution of its own. Work to determine how the various characters are correlated has been undertaken only recently.

In a negative sense, however, it is clear that groups exhibiting a relatively high degree of genealogical kinship are related to past and present ethnic groups only very remotely and in a highly complex manner. The evidence is particularly clear in the case of the "blood markers," whose heredity depends on specific genes. For example, the frequency of each of the genes on which the ABO system of blood groups depends (which has by now been studied fairly intensively) varies from region to region within the Arab world.[17]

The apparent physical characters, on which the

17. Concerning the theory of "populations" and the critique of traditional ideas, see Jacques Ruffié, *De la biologie à la culture* (Paris: Flammarion, 1977), pp. 375–418. As for the traditional ideas, a succinct and clear exposition that avoids the pitfalls of racism may be found in H. V. Vallois, *Les races humaines* (Paris: Presses Universitaires Françaises, 1944), Collection "Que sais-je?," no. 146.

usual classifications of the "races" are based, do,
under certain conditions and in a highly complex
fashion, reveal remote kinships. But none of these
characteristics has a geographical distribution that
coincides with that of Arab ethnos, however we
choose to define it.

This fact was obvious long before the discovery
of blood markers and the new school of "population" studies. The anthropologists were not remiss
in pointing this out, even if their warnings by and
large went unheeded. In the area covered by the
Arab ethnos, specialists identified several different
and markedly distinct "races." Most of these "races"
included both Arabs and non-Arabs. Thus some
researchers in North Africa linked many individuals to a so-called Ibero–Insular variant of a great
Mediterranean race. Others classified these human types as a subrace known as "Atlanto-
Mediterranean," a subdivision of the Mediterranean race, which also had representatives in the
peninsulas on the northern shore of the Mediterranean and even in the British Isles.

In the Near East several authors identified an
"Orientaloid" race where others saw only a "South
Oriental" subrace of the Mediterranean race. Some
held that an "Araboid" race was dominant in the
Arabian desert and in southern Iraq. In the Syrian
region "Armenoids" (or "Anatolians") were supposed to dominate, this group being a widely dispersed variant of the Dinaric race, itself (according
to some) a variant of the great Alpine race. In
Southern Arabia, along with Orientaloids and
Araboids and Veddoid or Gondoid elements re-

lated to certain Indian races, there were supposed
to be Armenoids. There, too, as throughout
Arabia, Egypt, and North Africa, were a good
many "Negroids" and "Ethiopoids."

We must stress that none of these more or less
artificial groups—the validity of which is being
undermined by recent research on blood
typology—represents a specific people. Even if it
were shown that an "Araboid" type, exhibiting a set
of apparent physical characteristics, was dominant
among the Arabian Arabs, this would not imply
that all of the latter were of this type, even in some
hypothetical past, nor would it rule out the occur-
rence of this type among other peoples. This is even
more true for the bulk of present-day Arabs,
among whom one can immediately spot a hundred
different physical types, merely confirming the results derived from the study of nonvisible characters.

Like most other peoples, then, the Arabs do not
constitute a physical "race" (or a genetically related
set of "populations"). The most that can be said in
this vein is that some physical characteristics, indicative in some highly complex way of possible
remote relationships, are prevalent in this or that
region within the Arab world, while others are absent or rare. If there is a unified people, that unity
does not rest on shared physical characters.

Ishmaelite Origin

Among Christians working for an "ecumenical"
reconciliation with Islam, and for reparation of the
historical wrongs done by Christendom to the

Muslims and particularly to the Arabs, much is often made of the fact that the Arabs are supposedly descendants of Ishmael, the elder son of Abraham by his servant Hagar, who was driven from his home at the insistence of Sarah, the patriarch's wife, after she had miraculously given birth to Isaac, an ancestor (through Jacob-Israel) of the Jews, and in particular of one of them, Jesus Christ (Genesis 16, 17, 21, 25). According to the book of Genesis, Ishmael, like all of Abraham's household, was circumcised before Isaac's birth. He was therefore a party to the first covenant between God and a particular human group, the covenant of circumcision. Certain of God's promises apply to him. From this a number of Christians have drawn conclusions as to the real, though limited, value of the divine revelation vouchsafed to Muḥammad, descendant of Ishmael; in the biblical story of the banishment of the servant woman and her son to the desert they see the theological "precursor," the metahistorical prefiguration of the destiny of the "outcasts" (from the Christian community)—the Muslims and the Arabs.[18]

This should be viewed as a modern adaptation of the conception of relations among ethnic groups that was worked out by the Semitic-speaking

18. The recent popularity of these ideas is due mainly to Louis Massignon, whose immense erudition and flashes of genius do not preclude a tendency to go beyond what is given in the texts with very bold interpretations that reflect his own passions and inclinations. Among recent authors who have elaborated on this theme, we shall cite only Michel Hayek, *Le mystère d'Ismaël* (Tours: Mame, 1964); *Les Arabes ou le baptème des larmes* (Paris: Gallimard, 1972); *D'Abraham à Mahomet: rupture et continuité* (announced but not yet in print as of 1978).

peoples, which we had occasion to mention earlier. Each group is supposed to have descended from an eponymous ancestor, and the genealogical affiliations of these ancestors represent the enmity or friendship, the more or less distant kinship felt to prevail among these groups at the time the genealogist set to work.

Similar genealogical theories were known to the ancient Babylonians, and we find abundant evidence of these in the ancient Israelite literature of which the Old Testament is an anthology. For the historian the stories in Genesis are a theory of this type, worked out in the first millennium B.C. or thereabouts by Israelite genealogists and perhaps indicative of the conceptions held by the tribes themselves. In any case, in the earliest of them Israel was regarded as being distantly related to certain Transjordanian tribes of the Negev and northwest Arabia; it forged ties either with one of them, probably the most important, or with a confederation, which bore the name "son of Ishmael." A fragment of the work of other Israelite genealogists, which also happens to have been preserved in Genesis, looks upon other Arabian tribes as descendants of Abraham by another woman, Keturah, probably symbolic of the lands of incense (Genesis 25:1–5).[19]

19. This is what seems to be indicated by the name of this woman, about whom no details are given. Concerning the nature of genealogical constructions of this kind, see the sound comments by Father R. de Vaux, *Histoire ancienne d'Israel, des origines à l'installation en Canaan* (Paris: Gabalda, 1971), vol. 1, pp. 157 ff. Cf. also I. Eph'al, "'Ishmael' and 'Arab (s)': a transformation of ethnological terms," *Journal of Near Eastern Studies* 35 (1976):225–35.

If, at the outset, the theory in question had some
basis in fact for the tribes involved, which belonged
to the group that would at a slightly later date be
called Arab, it was quickly forgotten along with
other such indigenous theories—all the more
readily so because the tribe or confederation bear-
ing the name of Ishmael merged with others or
assumed a new name, in any case vanishing from
sight. Among their Israelite neighbors, on the
other hand, the Ishmaelite theory was preserved
and consecrated by inclusion in sacred books,
which of course received wide diffusion later on.
The term Ishmaelite came to be used by the Jews as
a synonym for Arab, and pagan authors, instructed
by them, and later Christians, who inherited their
sacred books, adopted it. Alluding to the same
texts, the latter also named the Arabs Hagarenes,
"descendants of Hagar."[20]

At length this theory came back to the Arabs
themselves. No doubt the first to adopt it were
tribes in contact with the Judeo-Christian world,
which had in part accepted Christianity, Judaism, or Judeo-Christianity, as the fifth-century
Byzantine ecclesiastical historian Sozomenus tells
us.[21] But outside these peripheral tribes it had
very little currency. The name Ishmael (*Ismāʿil* in
Arabic) does not occur in the onomastic of central

20. The name Saracens (*Sarakēnoï*), which was most likely derived
from the name of a tribe that subsequently disappeared, was equally
popular as a term to designate the Arabs, beginning in the first centuries of Islam. It was completely unknown among the Arabs.

21. Sozomenus, *Ecclesiastical History* 6:38. In his view, it was the Jews
who apprised the Arabs of their Ishmaelite origins (which he, of
course, regards as their true origins).

Arabia during the period immediately prior to Islam. Its form is foreign to that onomastic—a foreign name, as the ancient Arab authors used to say.[22] Muḥammad was the first to adopt it and give it currency. Even so it was not taken very seriously at the outset. For several centuries the name Ismā'īl was given almost exclusively to children among the offspring of the Prophet.[23]

The biblical theory was fairly well brought into line with Arab traditions by the Arab genealogists of the first centuries of Islam. As we have seen, 'Adnān, the supposed ancestor of the northern Arab tribes, was made a descendant of Ishmael by his inclusion in one of several family trees. In any case the southern groups were excluded from Ishamel's posterity.

The notion that the Arabs descended from Ishmael is not mentioned in the Koran, which limits itself to placing Ismā'īl alongside his father Ibrāhīm (Abraham) at the time the latter built the Ka'ba in Mecca. Thus he plays an important role in classical Muslim doctrine according to which it was Abraham who brought monotheism to the Arabs. This monotheism is supposed to have been on the wane until it was revived by Muḥammad. For Muslims these are articles of faith. This idea, with Judeo-Christian roots, has been revived by recent Christian writers, bent on tying together the three

22. Jawālīqī, *Kitāb al-mu'arrab*, ed. A. M. Shākir (Cairo, 1361/1942), pp. 13 ff.

23. This is proven at length in the minutely detailed thesis of Father René Dagorn, *La geste d'Ismaël d'après l'onomastique et la tradition arabes*, as yet unpublished. I am making use of this work, along with the research that did in preparing a long introduction for this book.

monotheistic religions, thereby linking all of them
to the Abrahamic faith. Their motives are laudable
and generous. They may, as Massignon does, advance their thesis on a metahistorical plane. To do
so does not necessarily imply belief in an actual
genealogical descent, as was once credulously accepted. For the historian, the Arabs are no more
descendants of Ishmael, son of Abraham, than the
French are of Francus, son of Hector.

Conclusion: The Arab Ethnos

Many people think of and refer to themselves as
Arabs. Most but not all of them, and some others
besides, are regarded as Arabs by the rest. When
the question at issue is one of citizenship in a
nation-state, the law and the bureaucracy are there
to decide, and passports are issued to those who
meet certain strict, though changing, requirements
(cf. the series of laws concerning French nationality, for instance). By and large this settles the issue,
though public opinion does not always concur with
official definition, and in international law one en-
counters cases of people with double nationality or
without any nationality.

But when the question is one involving an
ethno-national group, there is no authority in
heaven or on earth to settle disputed cases. Where
the Arab group, for one, is concerned, these cases
are not few in number. The most we can do is to set
out in fairly clear terms the defining criteria of an
entity, a social group, which in actual fact functions, in certain respects at least, as a unit. At this
point one is forced to include within that entity

some individuals or groups that do not regard themselves as Arab, and to exclude some others that would like to be Arab. There are various grounds on which acceptance or rejection may be justified. Any definition of this kind involves a certain amount of arbitrariness, and the objective analyst can do no more than try to keep this to a minimum.

Within these limitations, we may consider members of the Arab ethnos, people, or nationality all those who:

1. speak a variant of Arabic *and* regard it as their natural language, the language they ought to speak, *or*, if they do not speak it, nevertheless have the same estimation of it;

2. regard as their patrimony the history and cultural traits of the people that has called itself and that others have called Arab, for whom one of those cultural traits has been, since the seventh century, belief in the Muslim religion (which is not limited exclusively to this people);

3. (what amounts to the same thing) claim Arab identity, possess an awareness of being Arab.

Though this definition is based on individual judgments, it is not a definition in psychological terms. These judgments are in fact conditioned by a concrete situation which is the product of social factors informed by thousands of years of history. Before Islam, what unified the tribes of the north and center of the Arabian peninsula was first of all linguistic and cultural bonds and, to a lesser degree, institutional ties. Afterward came temporary unification in a state under the ideological banner of Islam, which bound these tribes (and those of

Southern Arabia) together during the seventh and
eighth centuries. This was followed by the development of social and political conditions that made
possible the perpetuation and diffusion of the
Arabic tongue, which fostered an awareness of
being Arab among most of the tribes that continued in their traditional ways of life, and spread
such awareness to others, including some that had
adopted new ways of life. Similar conditions
gradually made it possible for people who had
adopted the Arabic tongue to share in this awareness to some degree. Finally, over the course of the
last two centuries, new conditions have brought
such awareness to many different elites and masses
within the confines of a fairly well-defined territory, among whom it took the form of a national
consciousness, a feeling of belonging to a unified
and specific cultural group destined to achieve
some form of political unity.

The question of the constitution of an Arab
ethnos may be fitted into the very broad context of
conditions under which similar kinds of bonds have
been formed among elementary social units, clans,
and tribes, ever since the end of the prehistoric
period. Fundamentally, these are economic conditions, for only with demographic growth,
emergence of a productive surplus available for
confiscation or exchange, and improved, speedier
communication does it become possible to overcome the isolation of the elementary groups.

Formations of this kind, whose geographical
distribution does not coincide with the boundaries
of any specific state, come in many varieties. From

the many words used to designate them we have chosen here the term "ethnos," rather than "people" or "nationality" (cf. German *Völkerschaft,* Russian *narodnost'*), on the grounds that, not being a word used in common parlance and hence relatively free of polysemic connotations, it is less likely to lend itself to confusion with similar concepts. One should be aware, however, that anthropologists sometimes use the term "ethnos" to refer to groups of a more special kind, culturally and linguistically homogeneous.

Once again, let us make clear that the ethnos is not to be confused either with a set of common physical characters resulting from genetic kinship ("race") or with a collection of common cultural traits ("civilization"). Groups defined by such criteria are generally multiethnic, while ethnic groups generally include people of different physical types and frequently admit a mix of various cultures.

⇒ 2 ⇐
The Nature and Growth of Arabhood

In this chapter we shall try to get an overview of the full extent of the present-day Arab ethnos. The ethnic history of each region will be briefly traced in order to throw some light on where each of the present Arab groups came from. It is wise to bear in mind that language is the most distinctive feature of the ethnos, even though it is not an absolute criterion. When we do not know what language was spoken by a people whose existence we know of either through archaeology or from the writings of other peoples (as is the case for the prehistoric period and frequently for the early parts of historical times), there is practically no way to attribute an identity to the group or to determine its social affiliations with other ethnic groups.

Bear in mind that such naïve questions as "What is the origin of this people? Where did it come from?" make almost no sense. All peoples are formed of a mixture of ethnic elements, and in most cases the constituents have often been present since prehistoric times. As a general rule what happens is that a relatively small contingent of immigrants with superior military forces conquers a region and assimilates its inhabitants. The prehistoric inhabitants of what is now France were conquered by the Gauls and thereafter became first Gauls, then Latins. The influence of a small number of conquerors led to the abandonment of the Gallic language. For a variety of sociological reasons, this rule no longer applied when France was subjected to later immigrations and conquests.

The Arab World

To begin with we shall look at what will here be called the Arab zone or world. By this we mean the group of states in which the Arab ethnos is dominant, and in which its language is the official state language in use by administrative officials who claim to be Arabs. This group constitutes a coherent geographical region, except for certain "de-Arabized" enclaves: the tiny state of Israel, and the two Moroccan cities of Ceuta and Melilla (Sabta and Malīla in Arabic), which have been Hispanicized for more than four centuries.

Arabia

The birthplace of the Arab people is the Arabian peninsula. It is presently divided into several states, all independent in theory, and all laying claim to Arabhood and giving voice to Arabism.

The Arabs of the peninsula (*jazīrat al-ʿArab*, "the isle of the Arabs," in Arabic) are for the most part descendants of members of the Arabic-speaking tribes of the pre-Islamic era. As we have seen, however, they were joined by the South Arabians, in small numbers in the few centuries prior to Islam, and on a large scale at the time of Islamization.

Most of these South Arabians were also connected with "tribes" (*sha'b* in South Arabian, a word which in Arabic has come to designate a "people"), though this association does not necessarily imply that they were nomadic shepherds. For the most part they were quickly Arabized. In the relatively inaccessible mountainous areas, however, as well as on the isolated islands and in coastal areas, isolated South Arabian communities continued to exist for a long time, and some are still to be found today.

These South Arabian communities include the whole of the Dhofar region, recently risen in revolt against the sultanate of Muscat and Oman, which claims to rule it (Dhofar has perhaps 150,000 inhabitants?); the island of Socotra and its neighboring islands (15,000 inhabitants), which are part of the People's Democratic Republic of Yemen (South Yemen); together with the groups adjacent to Hadramaut (the eastern part of the latter state) and in Oman to the east of Dhofar. Most the people who speak these dialects (called—mistakenly—Himyarite in Arabic) now also speak Arabic. This is the only language of culture they know, and the Dhofarian revolutionaries have made systematic efforts at Arabization, which for them is the equivalent of raising the level of literacy.

Foreign immigrants have always existed in Arabia, and the earliest of them became Arabized. Before Islam, the Ethiopians had penetrated South Arabia and even conquered it for a time; there were many Iranians in the east; and classical texts tell us of Greek colonies in the vicinity of Yemen. While many Arabian Jews in this period must have been Judaized natives, some had surely come from

Palestine. Christianity was spread primarily by the
Syrians. Black Africans and groups speaking the
Kushitic language, precursors of the present-day
Somalis, also must have been numerous.

Islam led to an increase in these immigrations by
encouraging a broad mixing of populations; one of
its institutions, the pilgrimage to Mecca, and its be-
stowal of prestige on the two holy cities, Mecca and
Medina, also contributed this mixing. Large colonies of Turks from central Asia as well as Indonesians grew up there. Slaves of various origins
were integrated into the population. Indian merchants set themselves up in the ports. Somalis,
Ethiopians, and Iranians continued to pour in.
Most of these elements were eventually Arabized.
Some tribes, which specialized in trades that were
held in contempt, are to this day considered to be
of foreign origin.

The limited modernization undergone by certain sectors of the economy in recent years has
brought subproletarians (along with craftsmen
and various specialists) into Saudi Arabia and the
tiny oil states of the Persian Gulf,[1] from Yemen and
the Sudan as well as countries such as Pakistan,
India, and Korea.

1. The name "Persian Gulf" has been in use since antiquity by Western geographers, and it was also taken up by Arab geographers in the
Middle Ages in the form *baḥr Fāris*, "Sea of Persis" (i.e., the Fārs
province of southern Iran). The Arab geographers sometimes extended the term to cover the entire Indian Ocean, which, however, was
usually known as *baḥr al-Hind*, "sea of India." Occasionally, a Persian
geography will refer to the "Gulf of Iraq." At present the Arabs have
taken to using the name "Arabian Gulf." To avoid getting involved in
this terminological controversy, based on nationalistic ideology, many
are now writing "the Gulf."

A rough and uncertain estimate has put the population of the peninsula at 17 to 20 million. Given the uncertainty of these figures, they may be taken also to represent the number of Arabs or Arabized persons.

The Fertile Crescent

The countries that form an arc around the Syro-Mesopotamian desert to the north of the Arabian peninsula have recently been baptized the Fertile Crescent. Traditionally, geography has distinguished the Syrian region (which from this point of view includes Lebanon, Palestine, and Transjordan) from Mesopotamia or Iraq. These fertile lands, significant as a cradle of agricultural economy and urban civilization, have been inhabited by Semitic-speaking populations since at least the third millennium B.C. From that time on, and even earlier, large-scale mixing of ethnic groups has taken place there. After the Assyrian and Babylonian conquests of the first half of the first millennium (accompanied by mass deportations), the region was unified politically under the great Persian Empire from 539 to 331 B.C. This was accompanied by still more intensive ethnic mixing, along with a linguistic unification—the entire Fertile Crescent adopted the Aramaic language, whereas the other Semitic languages of the region (Akkadian, Phoenician, Hebrew, etc.) fell into disuse. Alexander's conquest inaugurated a millennium of Hellenization. Greek and Macedonian colonies were established, and after A.D. 64, under the Roman Empire, there was an influx from all corners of that vast state. The Iranian states disputed the Roman claim to Mesopotamia and thereby fostered increased Persian immigration into the region. Greek was the dominant language among the wealthy and cultivated classes throughout this thousand-year-long period, but the masses continued to use Aramaic. Traits of Hellenic and Oriental culture mingled and contended with one another. The extent of the acculturation process varied widely from region to region.

By this time the Arab penetration had already begun, though today the hypothesis that the entire Semitic-speaking population of the Fertile Crescent came in wave after wave from Arabia is discredited. To the east and south of the Dead Sea, Arab tribes known as Nabataeans exerted pressure, at least as early as the seventh century B.C., on the people of Edom, looked upon by Israel as a fraternal rival. The Nabataeans absorbed the Edomites and founded the Nabataean kingdom, which Josephus and the Acts of the Apostles refer to as Arabia. This state adopted Aramaic and Greek as official languages, but its population was Arab. Annexed by Rome in A.D. 106, it became the Provincia Arabia. Farther north, the Arab infiltration was permanent. When the power of the states established by the sedentary peoples declined as the Seleucids fell into decadence, the Arabs who had infiltrated the region set up small kingdoms. One such was the Iturean dynasty of Ptolemy, son of Mennaeos, established at Chalcis ('Anjarr) in Coele Syria, the plain between the Lebanon and Anti-Lebanon mountain ranges, today known as the Beqā'; another was the dynasty of Samsigeram at Emessa (Homs). In upper Mesopotamia the Abgar dynasty at Edessa founded the kingdom of Osroëne and rapidly became Aramaized. Roman Syria was in part populated by Arabs. The emperor Septimius Severus married an Arab from Emessa, Julia Domna, whose sons and great-nephews ruled Rome. Somewhat later Philip the Arabian, from Shahba in Hauran, became Roman emperor from 244 to 249. In the Syro-Mesopotamian desert the caravan city of Tadmor (Palmyra), the birthplace of an ephemeral Palmyran Empire (circa 262–72), was Arab, even though it had adopted an Aramaic dialect (along with Greek) as its official language. In Mesopotamia there was one region sufficiently Arabized in the time of Xenophon, around 400 B.C., to be known as Arabia.

This penetration increased during the late Roman era and the Byzantine era. With the conquest of the country by the Muslim Arab armies between 633 and 643, the character of the penetration changed. As rulers guided by an ideology of their own, Islam, the Arabs were no longer absorbed by the settled population, which instead became Arabized. The large new cities (Kufa, Baṣra in Iraq) were at first (like Fusṭāṭ in Egypt and Kairouan in Tunisia) large encampments where Arabian Arabs congregated, along with their wives, children, and clients. They were also important markets, in which bargaining between city-dwellers and peasants took place in Arabic, which was also the language used in plantations in Iraq between Arab masters and their slaves. 'Abd al-Malik (635–705) made Arabic the administrative language.

Under the Abbasids (after 750) the Arabs and the earliest Arabized peoples ranged widely over the countryside. Conversion to Islam, which was by no means forcible, but which brought with it considerable financial and social advantages, also aided Arabization. Religious teaching, even when no better than cursory, brought with it some degree of familiarity with the Arabic text of the Koran. Conversion was often accompanied by the forging of a link with one of the Arab tribes through adoption.

Despite the rapid Arabization of the Fertile Crescent, some isolated Aramaic-speaking settlements held out for a long while in Lebanon, Anti-Lebanon, and northern Iraq. In the latter they are still important, but in Syria only three villages in the Anti-Lebanon mountains remain.

The following eventful years saw the penetration of the Fertile Crescent by a variety of ethnic elements, both because peoples living within the Muslim empire mingled with one another (some groups resettling far from their original location or moving at the behest of the sovereign) and because Turks, Kurds (Iranians), and Armenians invaded on a large scale. The states established by the Western crusaders between 1099 and 1291 were ephemeral, but many Franks married natives and some of their descendants were assimilated. There was a constant trickle of immigrants from the banks of the Mediterranean. Under the Ottoman Empire, the mingling that inevitably follows whenever new political boundaries are established around a vast area inhabited by many different peoples carried its effects into such remote areas as the Balkans. In the late nineteenth century the Muslim Circassians of the Caucasus, who were fleeing the Russian conquest, added still another patch of color to this variegated canvas.

Jewish immigration from many countries into Arabized Palestine, the ancestral holy land, had gone on virtually without letup, but the number of the pious determined to end their days near the theater of once and future theophanies was quite small. When Iberian Jews were expelled en masse in the late fifteenth century, many sought refuge in Ottoman toleration, and several thousand of them settled in Palestine. The slow immigration of ensuing centuries changed in character in the nineteenth century when the decline of the Ottoman Empire made (mainly Protestant) proposals for a Jewish state more plausible, at a time when anti-Semitic persecution had risen to dramatic new heights in Russia after 1881 and, most important of all, the Zionist movement was organized on firm foundations (1897), with the announced intention of making Palestine Jewish. This project, of course, came partially to fruition; the main stages in the creation of Israel were the Balfour declaration (1917); Jewish immigration under the British mandate in Palestine, which increased the Jewish population in the region from 11% to 31%; the UN decision to divide Palestine and the British withdrawal; the proclamation of the State of Israel (1948) and the ensuing war, which expanded its territory; and, finally, the June 1967 war, which led to the occupation of all Palestine up to the Jordan River, along with certain other territories. The October 1973 war again opened certain areas to Judaization, which since that time has also been on the rise in the regions conquered in 1967. Exile has of course dispersed the Palestinian Arabs over the adjacent countries and sometimes a good deal beyond. The loss of an Arab territory and its conversion into a foreign state are of course still contested by large numbers of Arabs, despite the recent willingless on the part of many Arab states (explicit or not) to resign themselves to the *de facto* situation.

Apart from the Israeli enclave, the Fertile Crescent includes a few other isolated non-Arab settlements. In Iraq (as in Iran and the U.S.S.R.) there are Christians (mainly Nestorians) who are called Assyrians and a few Jews who speak an eastern neo-Aramaic dialect. They number perhaps 35,000. Some 10,000 Mandeans speak another dialect belonging to the same group. The three Anti-Lebanon villages that still speak an Aramaic dialect number barely 4000 inhabitants. The Kurds, who speak an Indo-European language of the Iranian group, are said to number 2,000,000 in Iraq, 300,000 in Syria, and a few thousand in Lebanon. There may be 90,000 other Iranians in Iraq. The Circassians number perhaps 25,000 in Syria, 20,000 in Jordan, 8000 in Iraq; the Turks and Turkomans 35,000 in Syria, 100,000 in Iraq. Dispersed over the region are some tens of thousands of Gypsies, frequently Arabized. There are said to be 135,000 Armenians in Syria, 85,000 in Lebanon, 30,000 in Iraq.

All these figures are taken from estimates based on highly uncertain criteria and made at different times. The need for caution cannot be overstressed. Governments generally avoid furnishing ethnic or linguistic statistics for fear of providing ammunition to separatist movements. Conversely, these movements tend to overestimate the number of non-Arabs.

Many of the alien elements listed above are partially Arabized. In anti-Arab polemics it is not uncommon to see all these figures added together, inflated somewhat, and lumped with the confessional minorities to give a picture of a Fertile Crescent not in the least Arab. This picture is quite plainly distorted. The confessional minorities whose members speak Arabic do not cease to be Arab merely because they are not Muslim. Denominations such as "Greek Orthodox" should not be allowed to confuse the issue. The members of this religious group are Arabized Christians who observe Byzantine ritual and use Greek and Arabic in their liturgy. Conversely, we must point out that this ethno-linguistic Arabhood does not eliminate the problems alluded to above, the existence of which is all too readily denied by Arab nationalist ideology. The future of these problems is unpredictable. For the moment, however, only the Kurds and the Israelis impose limitations on the hegemony of the Arab ethnos in the Fertile Crescent.

Accordingly, out of 29.5 million inhabitants of the five states that make up the Fertile Crescent, we may count 22 million of them as Arabs.

Egypt

At least as early as the end of the fourth millennium B.C., the people of Egypt, who were the

product of prehistoric migrations and mingling
about which we shall never know in detail, adopted
a language that forms its own branch of the
Hamito-Semitic family. This was ancient Egyptian,
which in writing took the form of the so-called
hieroglyphics. For the period of antiquity we have
more detailed information about ethnic penetration of the region: Semitic-speaking western Asians
came from the east, Libyans and other elements
(certainly including many proto-Berbers) from the
west, blacks of various strains from the south, and
peoples from the Aegean and Mediterranean
shores from the north by sea.

   Superficially Hellenized, but also infiltrated by
Greek, Macedonian, Syrian, Jewish, and other colonists in the time of the Ptolemies and the Romans,
the Egyptians were called Qibṭ by the Arabs, Gebṣ
by the Ethiopians. This was a distortion of the
Greek name for Egypt (itself derived from the native name for the capital, Memphis) from which the
word "Copt" was taken. The developed form of the
ancient Egyptian language is likewise called Coptic
and was written with the Greek alphabet, to which
were added several letters adapted from ancient
writing. Despite intense pagan resistance, Christianity took firm root and cloaked itself in
specifically Egyptian forms. The Coptic Church
was the source of an abundant literature; largely
because of Egyptian nationalism it subscribed to
the monophysite tendency.

   Well before Islam the Arab penetration continued the steady infiltration of Semitic-speaking
west Asian populations across the Sinai desert and
the Red Sea. Herodotus (2:8) was already calling

the mountain range east of the Nile the "Arabian mountains." Strabo and Pliny placed Arab tribes between the Nile and the Red Sea. The city of Coptos, today called Qufṭ, in upper Egypt, is said to have been populated half by Egyptians, half by Arabs who came in the wake of other "Semites."

The Arab conquest of 640–41 radically altered the character of this infiltration. As in the Fertile Crescent, a slow process of Arabization got under way, to begin with in the vicinity of the large encampment at Fusṭāṭ (Old Cairo). But its speed picked up greatly with the immigration of a number of Bedouin clans and tribes from Arabia. These Bedouins, like their pre-Islamic predecessors, for a long time kept to the pastoral way of life in the deserts to the east and west, on the fringes of the cultivated area. The "Arabs" frequently rebelled and were brutally put down. Gradually, however, many of them took up sedentary ways and mixed with the native peasants, whom they helped to Arabize. The migration of large numbers of peasants to the big cities was also an important factor in Arabization. Islamization followed a parallel course but was guided by other laws. Here as elsewhere physical coercion was the exception and lasted only for brief periods. But the unseen pressure exerted by the social and particularly the financial advantages attaching to conversion to Islam worked its effects very slowly, though with steadily growing efficiency. The Copts, as those who remained Christians were henceforth called, long kept faith with their ancestral language. Coptic nonetheless fell into virtually total disuse as a common parlance in these countries after the year

1000. After the fourteenth century we find practically no copied manuscripts or engraved inscriptions in Coptic. Even Christian ecclesiastics composed their religious treatises in Arabic. Coptic subsisted only in the liturgy of the Egyptian Church, where it shared the honors with Arabic. It continued to be spoken in isolated villages (and perhaps in a few families elsewhere), the number of which declined steadily. Recently a village was discovered in which a few Coptic expressions survived in an otherwise Arabic dialect.

Egypt also received foreign immigrants during the Islamic era: with the Fatimid conquest in the tenth century came an influx of Berbers (who had always been present near the western border, where even today a Berber dialect containing many Arabic words is spoken in the Sīwa oasis); in the twelfth century many Kurds came with Saladin, as well as large numbers of soldier-slaves of Turkish and Circassian origin, the Mamelukes, who from the thirteenth century on became the ruling caste. Turkish and Circassian families still enjoy aristocratic status in Egyptian society. The steady flow of Armenians, Greeks, and Europeans to the cities reached considerable proportions after the sixteenth century, under Ottoman auspices. In the late nineteenth century the flow became a veritable flood, particularly under the British occupation (after 1881). The repercussions of Egypt's recovery of her independence in 1952 drove many of these foreigners out of the country.

Nearly all of today's 38 million Egyptians speak Arabic and may, according to the criteria given above, be considered members of the Arab ethnos. Whatever certain polemical writers may say on the subject, the Copts, or Egyptian Christians, are part of that group, even though some extreme Arab nationalists have questioned their fidelity to the nation and caused some problems for the Copts. Various estimates have been given of their number. Four million might be a reasonable approximation.

The Sudan

Lying to the south of Egypt, the region contained within the present borders of the state of Sudan[2] has since prehistoric times been a prime area for contact and intermingling between black-skinned ethnic strains and others more or less white-skinned concentrated to the north and east. The region has long been home to peoples speaking the Kushitic languages, which, along with the Semitic, Berber, and Egyptian groups, are included in the Hamito-Semitic family. These peoples may have held a preeminent place in the Meroitic kingdom during the second half of the first millennium B.C. But of this we are not certain. What we can say is that black-skinned elements have long been numerically dominant.

2. The name comes from the Arabic *bilād as-Sūdān*, "the land of the blacks." As the term indicates, it covered an area much broader than the present Sudan. In the twentieth century the name has been used to denote two different political entities, and care must be taken not to confuse them. In the east was the Anglo-Egyptian Sudan, which was supplanted by the Republic of the Sudan under discussion here. In the west was the French Sudan, an administrative subdivision of French West Africa, which became the Sudanese Republic (1958–60) and then adopted the name Mali.

Among these various populations were included, as early as the first century B.C., Arab tribes, if we are to believe the testimony of certain Greek and Latin writings. The great Muslim conquests of the eighth century did not carry beyond the southern border of Egypt. The Arabs concluded a lasting coexistence pact, the *baqt* (from the Latin *pactum,* the Greek *pakton*), with the kingdom of Makurra (whose capital was Dongola), which lay beyond the frontier. Like the kingdom of 'Alwa (capital Sōba) which lay farther to the south, this was a recently Christianized state whose dominant strata seem to have belonged to a Negroid ethnic group, the Nuba (from which comes the name Nubia). But Bedouin Arab tribes from Egypt gradually infiltrated the area, especially after the eleventh century. Muslim propaganda made major inroads from the fourteenth century. The kingdom of Dongola was destroyed in about 1350, that of 'Alwa in 1504.

In the sixteenth century, a group of Nilotic blacks, the Fung (or Funj), conquered the region, establishing what was called the kingdom of Sennar. They mingled with the Arabs (as well as with other already established populations) and were gradually Islamized. Their upper classes learned Arabic. The reigning dynasty established an Arab genealogy (Ummayyad) for itself. The Egyptian conquest (1820–22) increased somewhat the pace of Arabization and Islamization.

This conquest and its western and southern extension by the (Arab and European) rulers in Egypt's behalf established the present borders of the Sudan. They give official sanction to the hegemony of the Arab and Arabized (Muslim) populations of the north and center over the Kushitic-speaking Beja shepherds in the northeast and the ethnic groups that speak African Negro languages in the west and particularly in the south. This state of affairs has persisted throughout the changes in the Sudan's political situation: Egyptian colony until 1881, Mahdist state from 1881 to 1898, Anglo-Egyptian colony in theory but British colony in fact from 1899 to 1955, independent republic since January 1, 1956. Arabization has proceeded slowly. According to the 1956 census, 38.5% of the population claimed to be of Arab stock and 51.5% said that they spoke Arabic; both figures are probably exaggerated.

Independence brought to power an administration imbued with Arab nationalism, which systematized the efforts to Arabize and Islamize the south, where animistic and to a certain extent Christian faiths were prevalent. This policy, accompanied by brutal repression, provoked the bloody so-called Anyanya rebellion. In March 1972 this conflict was ended by an agreement which gave the south some degree of autonomy within the republic.

Taking demographic growth into account, it seems likely that out of some 16 million inhabitants of the Sudan in 1976, 7 to 8.5 million were Arabs. The southernmost limit of the Arab zone lies near the tenth (north) parallel. Farther north, however, there is a Beja center in the northeastern part of the country (640,000 in 1956), as well as areas in the northwest, west, and center where African Negro languages are spoken (1,256,000 at the same

date). At that time the population of the country
was 10,231,000.

North Africa

From the Sīwa oasis in western Egypt to the Atlantic Ocean stretches the vast area that was long
the preserve of the Berbers: Libya, Tunisia,
Algeria, Morocco. From archaeology and prehistoric anthropology we learn that there were migrations and minglings of peoples to whom we are
unable to attribute a linguistic identity. We do not
know what language was spoken by the blond and
blue-eyed "Libyans" who, in the predynastic era in
the late fourth millennium B.C., were neighbors on
the west of the Egyptians, with whom they fought
and also mingled after invading the northwestern
delta region. The Egyptians called them by a variety of names (Chehenu, later Chemehu, and much
later Meshwesh, followed, in the thirteenth century
B.C., by Lebu, which is the equivalent of Libyans)
which probably referred to different groups. However, as reflected in Egyptian texts, particularly
during the period when Libyan pharaohs ruled
Egypt (circa 950–700), some of the words used by
these peoples seem to have been Berber. By this
date a core ethnos that spoke one of the Libyo-
Berber dialects (one of four branches of the
Hamito-Semitic family) must have spread out over
a wider area. We do not, and probably never will,
know either the location of its "original" dwelling
place or the date it moved away and broke off from
the even more ancient core group that spoke the
common ancestor of all these languages, about
whose geographical and chronological particulars

we are also in the dark. In any case, the "Libyo-Berbers" followed the general rule of assimilating, destroying, or subjugating all preexisting populations in this immense region.

The Phoenician (Carthaginian or Punic) and Greek colonists of the first millennium B.C. brought only marginal changes to the ethnic composition of the region. Cyrenaica was Hellenized. The peoples described by Greek and Latin writers beginning in the third century B.C.—Moors in Morocco, Masaesyli and Massyli (or Numids) in Algeria, Gaetuli in the south—were certainly Berbers, and it is probably their language that we find in the Libyan inscriptions, the oldest of which are said to date from the second century. Under the Roman Republic and Empire, which gradually annexed all these countries between the second century B.C. and the middle of the first century A.D., the use of Latin became widespread in the administration, in law, and in the army. Thorough Latinization, however, was limited to an area from which Punic seems to have disappeared. Berber was to remain the everyday language of the natives, the only one spoken by the peasants and shepherds. Beginning at least as early as 250 there were continual Berber rebellions which must have limited the influence of Latin still more.

The Arabs conquered what is now Libya in about 642–43. The conquest of the remainder of the Byzantine and Berber Maghrib, begun in 647, was complete slightly after 700. Arabization and Islamization then began along the same lines as had been followed in the East, to begin within the vicinity of the Kairouan encampment. But it ran into far stronger resistance from the Berbers. They put up a ferocious struggle against the invading armies, fighting as members of free tribes and showing far more determination than the subjects of the despotic states of the Near East, who are already ideological dissidents. Defeated and presumably subdued and Islamized, they carried on the struggle by joining dissident Muslim movements, sometimes called heresies, which even under Arab rule fostered particularism. Arabization made headway around the middle of the eleventh century with a large-scale influx of Arab tribes from the east. At about the same time began the era of Berber dynasties led by native rulers, who preached religious reform: first the Almoravids (around 1060–1145), and later the Almohades (around 1145–1269) and their successors. These rulers even used the Berber tongue at times to spread their propaganda.

In the Ottoman era (sixteenth to nineteenth century) Berber still retained some influence in a largely Arabized Libya. The rule of Istanbul over Algeria and Tunisia was tenuous. But a Turkish-speaking oligarchy, whose ranks were swelled by Europeans and Christian Levantines converted to Islam, was predominant, while Arabization of the countryside proceeded more or less generally. Morocco, as well as Mauritania, escaped Ottoman domination. The Moroccan dynasties claimed to be descended from the Prophet, hence of Arab origin, but Berber linguistic influence in the country continued to be considerable.

The French colonization of the Maghrib and the

Italian colonization of Libya (which got under way between 1830 and 1912, depending on the country) brought a large influx of European colonists. But they mingled little with the Arab-Berber population, and most of the foreigners left these countries when they won their independence, between 1951 and 1962.

The present ethno-linguistic situation is complex. Objective inquiry into the reality of what is, of course, a changing situation has been impeded by the political purposes to which the particular interests of the Berber-speaking population were put by the colonial powers in the past, and by denial of those interests in the name of Arabist ideology in the present. It should be emphasized that many Arabs in these regions today are Arabized Berbers mingled with descendants of Arabian Arabs and others. There have even been instances of Berberized Arabs. Speaking a dialect of Arabic or Berber does not necessarily or invariably imply acceptance of corresponding ideologies of ethnic identity or specific cultural traits. The numbers of the bilingual are legion. Classical Arabic is everywhere the only language of culture. The Berber dialects are not as a rule written down. The speaker of Berber normally regards Arabic as his "official" language, much as the Bretons or Basques until recently regarded French, and in large part still do. To the foreigner, speakers of Berber will frequently declare themselves to be Arabs.

The eastern outpost of the Berber language is the Sīwa oasis in western Egypt (4000 inhabitants?). Berber is said to be spoken by upwards of 55,000, perhaps, in Libya. In Tunisia six villages of the isle of Djerba and seven on the continent in the southern part of the country yield some 20,000 Berber speakers, some of whom have held on to their language even after moving into the cities, quite often for use as a secret tongue. Algeria boasts a much higher proportion of Berber speakers, said to be as high as 30%, which at present would mean upwards of 5,500,000. They are concentrated mainly in Kabylia in the north and in the Aurès mountains to the southwest. It was once calculated that they constituted 38% of the population in the former Constantine department, 37% in the Algiers department, and 10% in Oran. In Morocco estimates have put the Berber-speaking population at 40% of the total, which would give about 7 million at present. This seems high, but it is politically impossible to obtain statistics on the matter. In any case large numbers of these Berber speakers also speak Arabic. The Sahara is largely populated by speakers of Berber.

Here we put our finger on the ambiguity of the first item in our definition of the Arab ethnos (p. 45 above). Many Berber speakers today apparently consider Arabic the language they ought to speak and regard it as their "natural" language, the one they would "ordinarily" speak if they were sufficiently cultivated, high on the social scale, etc. This does not (not necessarily, at any rate) prevent their being attached to their Berber dialect, which they also regard as their "natural" language, the one they "ordinarily" speak in the dealings of everyday life as well as for the enjoyment of its oral literature. On the whole, this complex situation is not very different from that of the Welsh in Britain, or the Provençal regionalists in France, prior to the advent of full-fledged separatist nationalist movements.

This presents us with a delicate problem in estimating the size and extent of the Arab ethnos. If recognition of the Arabic tongue is deemed the sole linguistic criterion for membership in the political entity in question, virtually all the Berber speakers must be granted membership in the Arab ethnos, which would swell its ranks by 44.5 million (minus some 270,000 Europeans), the entire population of this region. If the mother tongue and common parlance are taken as criteria, a deduction of some 10 million ethnic Berbers must be made. Then, too, in the light of other examples it is not out of the question that future political developments may lead at least some of the Berber speakers to make a more definitive choice in favor of one ethnic group or the other.

Mauritania

Paradoxically, Mauritania, which lies as far from Arabia as one can possibly get in the Arab world, is strongly reminiscent of Arabian living conditions and social and ethnic structures. But the country was for a long time populated by black Africans, who were driven out by Berber invasions from the north. When these began is not known, but they were heightened at any rate by the Arab conquest of North Africa in the seventh century. The Berber infiltration was fairly slow, and Islamization came only in the eleventh century, not without persistent opposition. Beginning in the fourteenth century Arab infiltration seems either to have begun or to have increased in southern Morocco, particularly with the Ma'qil tribe, which had come originally from Arabia. Widespread Arabization of the Berber tribes took place in the following centuries amid complex factional struggles involving coalitions of Arabic- and Berber-speaking groups, out of which emerged the Arab-dominated emirates and the Marabout groups, which invoke Islamic or Arabist ideologies.

Thus at present a majority of Mauritanians belongs to the Arab ethnos. The last remaining group of Berber speakers recently disappeared. Out of a population of 1,320,000 (1976 estimate), there are many blacks, particularly in the south, who speak Wolof, Peul, or Sarakolle. No statistics have been published. Figures of 20% to 30% of the population are mentioned. The blacks claim that the figure should be nearer 50%.

The one-time Spanish Sahara (population approximately 117,000), which lies between Morocco and Mauritania, was in 1975 officially divided between those two countries. But the natives of the region (Arabs or Arabized Berbers except for a minority of approximately one-quarter of the total consisting of black Africans who often describe themselves as Arabs), who had formed a popular liberation front to fight the Spanish (Polisario Front), have challenged this settlement and with Algerian support have set up the Democratic Saharan Arab Republic, which is claiming independence.

Fringe Areas and Isolated Arab Communities

The zone occupied by the Arab ethnos does not, obviously, coincide with recognized political boundaries. Inside but at the edges of what we have been calling the Arab zone, Iraqi Kurdistan and southern Sudan are inhabited by other ethnic groups. Depending on how one views the complex question of the identity of the Berber speakers, one may or may not wish to include the Berber-dominated regions of North Africa. On the other hand, Arabs are found beyond the borders of the Arab states. We shall refer here to the areas into which Arab populations have spread beyond the frontiers of the Arab zone as the Arab fringe areas, and along with these we shall also discuss several isolated communities even more remote from the Arab heartland, cut off from the region of Arab rule by areas of different ethnic character.

The Asiatic Fringe

In Turkey there are said to be approximately 370,000 speakers of Arabic (1965 figure). As to their distribution we are largely in the dark. Many of them merely represent the extension of the Arab ethnos into a thin strip along the northern frontier of Syria and somewhat beyond in the direction of Cilicia. In the former *sanjak* of Alexandretta (Is-kandarun in Arabic, in Turkish spelling Iskende-run), a part of Syria under the French mandate after 1918, lived a mixed population of Arabs and Turks. France (in the face of Syrian opposition) ceded this district to Turkey to all intents and purposes in 1937, at first as an autonomous region (called Hatay) with a special international status sanctioned by the League of Nations. In 1939 it became an integral part of Turkey. Statistics concerning the relative proportions of different languages and ethnic groups in this region were particularly dubious and often challenged. In any case, the nationalist policies followed by the various governments did all that could be done to bring the ethnic structure of the population into line with political boundaries.

The Arab presence in Iran is of long date. It began certainly before Islam, notably when certain Arab tribes occupied a large portion of Mesopotamia, which has generally been included within the Iranian states since the sixth century B.C. No frontier could check the eastward push of these tribes. In the seventh century A.D., Iran was conquered and experienced the wholesale mingling of populations that took place within the Islamic empire and its successors. Arab tribes settled in all the countries of the empire. The transfer of political power to Turko-Iranian dynasties and the perpetuation of the power of the important Iranian landowners ensured that many of these Arabs would gradually come under Iranian influence. But there were more recent Arab immigrations, along with a slow but steady influx of nomads, sailors, and merchants along the southern coast, which began before Islam and has continued ever since. In the 1950s it was estimated that there were 1,200,000 Arabs on the southern coast. Some Arab-speaking tribes, however, may be found farther inland, along with others that are considered, and consider themselves, Arabs, though they speak a dialect of Persian. Arabs are particularly numerous in the southwest, in Khuzistan province on the Iraqi border, which was long known as Arabistan, "the land of the Arabs." They were politically influential in this area, and the region is presently the object of Arab nationalist claims.

We might also include in this Asiatic Arab fringe the Cypriot Christians who came from the Arab Levant originally, mainly of Lebanese Maronite origin; their number was put a decade ago at 3000 or so. They are presently almost completely Hellenized and speak a Greek Cypriot dialect. In one village of some 1000 inhabitants (now in the Turkish zone) Arabic is still spoken, except by the younger generation, which is completely Hellenized.

Isolated Communities in the Turko-Iranian Zone

In Soviet central Asia and Afghanistan, amid the Turkish and Iranian populations, there are still some groups that claim to be Arabs and are considered as such. It is by no means certain that they are linked to the earliest Arab colonists from the time of the great conquests, who were rapidly Iranized. They may well be immigrants who made their way to their present home by stages, the last being the cities and countryside of Iran itself. Evidence of their presence dates back as far as the sixteenth century. There are said to be about 8000 Arabic speakers in Uzbekistan and Turkmenistan (according to the 1959 census figures, which show a decrease compared with earlier figures). There may be a thousand or so others in the Dagestan A.S.S.R. in the Caucasus. In northwest Afghanistan

there are Persian-speaking groups that claim to be
Arab, along with a few villages in which Arabic is
spoken. The figure of 25,000 Arabs has been put
forward for this country.

East Africa

Arab and especially South Arabian colonization
of the coast of east Africa began well before Islam.
In the second or third century a considerable portion of the coastal area of present-day Tanzania
was governed (according to a Greek text entitled
Periplus of the Eritrean Sea) by an official delegated
by the viceroy of the Ma'āfir district in Yemen. The
sailors of the Arabian coast had always plied the
Red Sea and even ventured into the Indian Ocean.
What is more, migration in the opposite direction
was just as common.

This partly accounts for the Arab settlement
of the Sudan. Arabian Arabs and particularly
Yemenis pushed into Eritrea (presently a province
of Ethiopia) along the coast, while Sudanese Arabs
made inroads from the northwest, mainly to sell
their wares. The prestige of the language of Islam
among the Eritrean Muslims (more than half,
perhaps as much as two-thirds of the population),
the diversity of languages spoken, and the many
Arab peddlers have made Arabic a language of
daily use for a considerable number of Eritreans
(presently 15–20% of the population, according to
G. A. Lipsky). In 1952 the Eritrean government
declared Arabic and Tigrinya official languages.
Totally integrated into Ethiopia in 1962, this region saw the development of an Eritrean separatist
movement—a movement supported by certain

Arab countries and strongly influenced by Arab nationalism—which has further increased the prestige of Arabic and may help to make the language still more widely spoken.

Elsewhere in Ethiopia we find Arab colonies (of merchants in particular) in Harar, Jimma, and some small cities. For the same reasons as in Eritrea, Arabic is a *lingua franca* in the southwestern districts around Jimma. The many Ethiopian Muslims sometimes have a rudimentary knowledge of the tongue. Estimates of the numbers of Arabs in all of Ethiopia vary from 15 to 50 thousand or so. These figures are very rough.

Somalia, too, has long attracted Arab immigrants, particularly from the southern part of the peninsula (even recently there were tiny groups that spoke South Arabian dialects in the area). The number of Arabs in Somalia has been put at some 30,000. There are said to be 15,000 in the new Republic of Djibouti.

Farther south, the coast of Kenya and Tanzania, like the Somalian coast, has long received a fairly considerable influx of Arabs. Local Arab traditions confirm the testimony of the *Periplus of the Eritrean Sea* concerning pre-Islamic South Arabian settlement in this region. The already settled colonists later converted to Islam and were joined over the centuries by waves of Muslim immigrants consisting of Arabian Arabs (mainly from the southern part of the peninsula, particularly Hadramaut and Oman), Persians, Indians, Syrians, and others. These were merchants involved in the brisk trade linking Asian and African coasts of the Indian Ocean. An Arab aristocracy ruled the commercial cities of the coast and had little interest in relations with the inland areas. Islamization of the blacks nevertheless made some headway, and a specific culture grew up with its own language, Swahili ("coastal"), a Bantu tongue incorporating many Arabic words. In the seventeenth century the sultanate of Muscat, at Oman in southeastern Arabia, formed an alliance with all the Arab colonies of what was called Zanjebār, the black slave coast (whence the name Zanzibar). In the nineteenth century the sultan of Muscat also reigned over this region, which prospered thanks to the ivory and slave trades; he established large plantations. The coastal Arabs pushed farther and farther inland. English and German colonization put an end to this development in the 1880s. Decolonization came in 1961–63.

At present there are said to be around 30,000 Arabs in Kenya, mainly in the coastal province, and perhaps 30,000 in Tanzania. In the sultanate of Zanzibar, which has been independent since December 1963, the well-to-do Arab and Muslim aristocracy was toppled from power by the bloody revolution of January 12, 1964. With the transfer of power to an extreme left-wing government made up predominantly of Africans, many Arabs left the islands. Zanzibar joined with Tanganyika in a state that took the name Tanzania, within which Zanzibar retained some degree of autonomy.

The Central and West African Fringe Areas

Here as in the east, the Arab ethnos has overflowed the borders of the countries that make up what we are calling the Arab zone. In the west only very small groups of Arabs are actually found south of those borders: some 50,000 "Moors" (i.e., Mauritanian Arabs or Arabized peoples who speak the dialect of that country, Ḥassānīyah), who have either settled in Senegal or who wander from one country to the other, and 15,000 others in Mali along the Mauritanian border. In Niger some 10,000 Arabs look principally to Chad for guidance, besides which there are a few recent immigrants from Algeria.

Chad, which borders on two Arab countries, Libya to the north and Sudan to the east, is the major Arab center in the region. Indeed, there may be as many as 400,000 (some say 700,000) Arabs in this country, concentrated in the north and the east, with a few thousand more settled in the capital. Raising livestock for a livelihood, these tribes are usually referred to by their neighbors as Showa, which means shepherds, although their herds consist mainly of dromedaries and bovidae. They came to their present home in successive waves beginning at least as far back as the fourteenth century, from Libya and primarily from the Sudan.

The European Fringe:
The De-Arabized Regions and Malta

At the time of the great conquests the Arab ethnos spread north of the Mediterranean. Spain, conquered between 711 and 714, was partially Arabized (and Berberized). Many natives converted to Islam and forged links with the Arabs, here as elsewhere. But Romance dialects continued to be spoken (and ultimately were written down in Arabic script) alongside Arabic, even by Arabized Muslims. The Christian reconquest, which began to score major victories from the eleventh century on, resulted in the incorporation of many speakers of Arabic into the Christian states. With the fall of the last Muslim state, the kingdom of Granada, in 1492, the Arabic language fell into disuse among the Muslims who remained in Spain, the Mudejars, who were forcibly converted to Christianity in 1502 and officially forbidden to use Arabic in 1567. The crypto-Muslim "Moriscos" who were not assimilated were finally expelled in 1611.

Sicily, conquered between 827 and 965, was Arabized and Islamized before being recaptured by the Normans between 1070 and 1085. A considerable portion of the population continued to speak Arabic and to adhere to the Muslim faith for a time, but Islam and Arabic both gradually disappeared. Sicilian dialect has retained some Arabic words.

In Malta and Gozo, on the other hand, which were conquered in the late eighth or the ninth century and recaptured by the Normans in 1090, Islam may have disappeared after 1249, but an Arabic dialect is still spoken by the mass of the population (of approximately 330,000). The staunchly Catholic Maltese are concerned to play down the Arabic nature of this dialect, which since the eighteenth century has been written in Latin script and called "Maltese." Its origin is commonly said to be composite, but it is basically a Maghrib-type dialect of Arabic, though it does contain a relatively high proportion of Italian loan-words.

The Diaspora

Under the conventional term "diaspora" we shall place individuals and groups belonging to the Arab ethnos who reside (temporarily or permanently) in areas geographically separated from the coherent region in which the Arab ethnos is dominant, i.e., the countries of the Arab zone and its fringe areas. Actual cases are always quite complex, and the dividing line between isolated communities in the fringe area and communities in the diaspora is not a sharp one. If we gave particular prominence above to certain of these isolated communities, this was because they appeared to be stable, with Arab elements enjoying long-established positions in avowedly multiethnic societies. The term diaspora, on the other hand, carries with it more of a connotation of instability. In many societies Arab elements, often remarkably well-adapted, pretend that their presence is only temporary, and that eventually they aim to achieve complete assimilation or to return to the country of their birth. In general we are concerned with individuals who, after private deliberation, have decided to emigrate, though in many cases powerful indirect compulsions may well have brought many individuals to the same decision. By contrast, the settlement of the Arab zone and its fringe areas was by and large the result of collective decisions taken by ethnic groups or ordered by the authorities.

Modern conditions, however, can change the

picture completely. For one thing, industrial society fosters more complete assimilation and mixing.
A countervailing factor is that ease of communication encourages émigrés to maintain contact with
their native land. Then, too, the ascendancy of
nationalist ideology works against assimilation and
impels governments to do all within their power to
maintain control over their émigré nationals.

Arab emigration has a long history. We know of
Arab and South Arabian migrants in antiquity, for
the most part merchants hawking their wares in
Greece and Egypt. Despite Christian hostility, there
were some individual Muslim Arab immigrants in
medieval Europe, on a temporary or more lasting
basis. In modern times some Arabic-speaking
Christians, especially Lebanese, have emigrated
voluntarily. Simultaneous individual emigration on
a large scale was found, however, only among the
Arab descendants of the South Arabians of antiquity, the people of Oman, Hadramaut, and
Yemen, who went mainly to east Africa and India,
Malaysia, and Indonesia. These were for the most
part merchants, who set up shop in the new lands,
and now and then also soldiers, who served as
bodyguards of local potentates. They married local
women and fathered castes of half-breeds, who are
said to have made up one-fifth of the population of
the ports on the Malabar coast in the sixteenth
century, to cite one instance. But often they re-
turned to their homelands (a similar case is recorded in the *Thousand and One Nights*), and the influence of Indian and Indonesian "blood" on the
physical type of the South Arabian populace is

today detectable by the naked eye. This emigration increased considerably after the eighteenth century. In 1937 Indonesia counted some 71,000 Arabs.

Syrian and Lebanese emigration began mainly in the late nineteenth century, stimulated by the hatred felt (particularly by Christians) for the despotic regime of the Ottoman sultan 'Abd ul-ḥamīd. Most of the émigrés headed for the American continent, which at the beginning of this century was receiving 20,000 immigrants a year from this area. In 1939 the number of immigrants in all the Americas was put at 600,000. This diaspora played a considerable role in the economy of Latin America. Its thought and literature were quite influential in the Arab world. In the period ending in 1929, no fewer than 268 Arabic periodicals, including 205 newspapers, were published in the Americas. In 1950 it was estimated that there were 450,000 United States citizens of Arab origin. In 1975 there were said to be 400,000 Lebanese in the United States, 300,000 in Brazil, and 313,000 in the rest of the Americas (very high figures have been put forward for Brazil and Argentina in particular), plus 98,000 in Africa, where émigrés have long made their livings as merchants, large and small, and as usurers.

The two major factors in Arab emigration at present are importation of relatively unskilled laborers by industry and industrialized agriculture in the developed countries, and the "brain drain." In the first case, the immigration is usually seasonal or temporary, though certain individuals may decide to stay on permanently. In France, for example, most of these immigrant workers are North Africans; there is an increasing tendency to allow them to bring their families with them. As of January 1, 1974, the number of Algerian, Tunisian, and Moroccan nationals in France was estimated at 1,260,000 (of whom 600,000 worked) out of a total of slightly more than 4 million foreigners. But there were also nearly 250,000 French citizens of Algerian origin. By the end of 1977 statistics showed 1,405,422 Arabs of all nationalities in France.

The brain drain obviously involves fewer individuals, but its qualitative importance is considerable. Conditions unfavorable to intellectual work and low pay in this sector in the underdeveloped countries, political events (exodus of people linked in one degree or another with colonial regimes, political opponents, members of classes expropriated by the government in countries with state-controlled economies, etc.) and tempting offers from the industrialized nations, have all conspired to drive many intellectuals from their homelands.

The consequence of all the political and social upheaval has been to make émigrés of people victimized by the new regimes and dissatisfied with or fearful of the results of the turmoil. Most recently this has happened with the Lebanese civil war, which began in 1975.

The number of Arabs spread throughout Europe and America, not to mention sub-Saharan Africa and eastern Asia, by the workings of these various processes is impossible to determine, in view of the difficulty of obtaining statistics and the inadequacy of the figures available. Account must be taken not only of those who are still legal aliens in their host countries but also of those who have obtained citizenship, in some cases long ago. Statistics on the latter category are sorely lacking. The number of immigrant workers is subject to rapid fluctuations. The currently available estimates on which the table below is based are highly uncertain but give some idea for the moment at least of orders of magnitude. The Arab émigrés themselves speak of 90,000 Arabs in Canada and 100,000 in Chile, for example. The largest concentration in North America is said to be in Detroit, where there are supposedly 80,000 Arabs.

Size of the Arab Ethnos

The table in the following pages should be regarded as providing no more than rough indications of orders of magnitude. Total population figures marked with asterisks are even more dubious than other estimates. All the data are taken from generally reliable works based on figures worked out for the most part between 1970 and 1977. Most of the Arab population figures are, as has been mentioned, crude estimates, often quite arbitrary. In addition, they are frequently dependent on the criteria chosen to define the ethnos, particularly the extent to which speakers of Berber are included or not. For example, it would be possible to eliminate Malta entirely by changing the criteria.

Table 1

Size of the Arab Ethnos

Country (in thousands)	Total Population (in thousands)	Arab Population
1. The Arab Zone		
A. *Arabia*		
Saudi Arabia	8,970*	8,700
Kuwait	1,030	750
Bahrain	260	210
Qatar	140*	60
United Arab Emirates	350*	100
Muscat and Oman	790*	750
North Yemen	5,000	4,900
South Yemen	1,750*	1,600
Total	18,290	17,070
B. *The Fertile Crescent*		
Iraq	11,510	8,600
Syria	7,600	6,900
Lebanon	3,000*	2,400
Jordan	2,780	2,500
Israel	3,500	540
Territories occupied by Israel	1,120	1,120
Total	29,510	22,060
C. *The Nile Valley*		
Egypt	38,070	37,900
Egyptian territories occupied by Israel	30	30
Sudan	16,130	7,700
Total	54,230	45,630

Table 1 continued

D. *North Africa*

Libya	2,440	2,360
Tunisia	5,740	5,380
Algeria	18,250	12,500
Morocco	17,830	12,000
Ceuta and Melilla	162	7
ex-Spanish Sahara	117	95
Total	44,539	32, 342

E. *Mauritania*

Mauritania	1,320	1,100
Total in the Arab Zone	174,889	118,202

2. Fringe Areas and Isolated Communities

A. *Turco-Iranian Region*

Turkey	40,167	370
Iran	33,400	1,500
Cyprus	640	4
Afghanistan	19,800*	25
U.S.S.R.:		
Uzbekistan	13,085	
Turkmenistan	2,394	8
Dagestan	1,500	1
Total	110,986	1,908

B. *East Africa*

Ethiopia	28,680*	35
Somalia	3,260*	30
Djibouti	106*	15
Kenya	13,850	35
Tanzania	15,610	30
Total	61,506	145

Table 1 continued

C. *West and Central Africa*		
Senegal	5,110*	50
Mali	5,840	15
Niger	4,730	10
Chad	4,120	500
Total	19,800	575
D. *Europe*		
Malta and Gozo	300	300
Total Fringe Areas and Isolated Communities	192,592	2,928
3. Diaspora		
Europe		1,400
Asia		100
Africa		100
America		1,200
Oceania		30
Total		

Summary of the Arab Population

Arab Zone	118,202
Fringe Areas and Isolated Communities	2,928
Diaspora	2,830
Total	123,960
or roughly 3.1% of the world's population.	

Sources: *World Bank Atlas;* various U.N. publications; Y. Courbage and Phillipe Fargues, "La population des pays arabes d'Orient," *Population* 30 (1975):1111 ff.; J. M. Cuoq, *Les musulmans en Afrique* (Paris: Maisonneuve et Larose, 1975); U. Geiser and H. Steffen, *Population Distribution . . . in the Yemen Arab Republic* (Berne: Swiss Technical Cooperation Service); and San'ā', Central Planning Organization, 1977, etc.

3

Arabism

Distinct from the vague awareness of membership in the Arab group, from Arabhood, and from the ethnonational ideology it engenders, but based upon that ideology, "Arabism," as we shall call it in these pages, is an Arab nationalism related to the modern form of nationalism that has slowly evolved in Europe since the end of the Middle Ages. The growth of national markets gave a tremendous, unprecedented strength to the network of relations by which the different parts of the ethno-national group were tied together. The bourgeoisie, which played an especially important role in this integration, developed an extensive ideology that stressed the necessity and primacy of the new state organisms. The bourgeoisie wanted a powerful state which would guarantee individual freedom; appeal was made, vaguely at first, to the concept of the sovereign will of the people, most clearly defined within the newly risen strata and expressed through parliaments and estates general. These bodies mobilized vague feelings of identity—implicit or latent in the populace—and therefore required the allegiance of the lower classes. Accordingly, little by little the concept of the nation-state was worked out by intellectual theoreticians. It slowly gained legitimacy. After its success in Europe and America it was adopted by the elites in colonized countries, who made similar use of the concept in mobilizing their masses against foreign domination. The theoretical controversy between those who see this as the borrowing of a European ideological model superimposed on a different reality and those who believe that it was an idea spontaneously generated by local conditions is idle. The European ideological model was adopted because it corresponded best to the requirements of situations obtaining in the Third World in the twentieth century, and, as in Europe, that model relied on the spontaneous emotions of the masses.

Arabism, or Arab nationalism, grew up slowly in response to situations and events for which theory provided a series of approximate accounts; these theoretical descriptions were at first quite crude. It is best, therefore, to examine the growth of Arabism in its historical context.

Muslim Protonationalism and the
Birth of Arabist Ideology

Mention has already been made of the earliest traces of the idea that it was the vocation of all Near Eastern Arabs to establish a specifically Arab state. Hostility to Turkish power had slowly and obscurely given rise to awareness of an Arab identity in the portion of the Near East that was under the direct authority of Istanbul—Arab Asia— where that awareness had to compete with the still powerful feeling of Muslim community that united Arabs and Turks. It took a long time for an organized, coherent, explicit ideology of the Arab nation—an Arab nationalism—to develop and attract an audience of any size. The first nationalism to emerge was more in the nature of a (Muslim and Ottoman) protonationalism in an antiimperialist key, whose target was European imperialism.

Over the course of the nineteenth century the Western powers increasingly asserted their hegemony over the Ottoman Empire. European ambassadors dictated the policy of the sultans and forced the opening of Eastern markets to European products. The political and economic subjugation of the Ottoman East provoked certain reactions. The rulers envisaged reform from above, while intellectuals pressed for a more radical attitude—and to begin with for westernization, pure and simple.

But the catastrophic consequences of the application of economic liberalism to the Ottoman Empire, the implementation of European imperialist plans, and the contempt shown by the Western powers for internal reforms led to disillusionment and a change of heart on the part of Muslim intellectuals. Particularly after the occupation of Tunisia by France (1881) and of Egypt by Great Britain (1882), protests against European imperialism crystallized around the Muslim community and the Ottoman Empire, the last Muslim state to remain intact and relatively powerful. A new type of intellectual conceived of both the community and the Empire on the model of a European nation. As caliph and sultan, ʿAbd ul-ḥamīd (1878–1908) exploited this tendency for despotic, reactionary, and obscurantist purposes.

The great ideologue of this antiimperalist, pro-tonationalist protest movement—after the Turkish poet Namïq Kemāl, who developed similar ideas in 1871–76—was the Persian Jamāl ad-dīn, known in-correctly as al-Afghāni, "the Afghan" (1839–97). Activist, revolutionary conspirator, sower of ideas, and deist free-thinker, he was won over to the use of Islam (i.e., in the sense of Muslim community) for tactical purposes in about 1880. His anti-imperialist, pan-Islamic outlook did not prevent him from supporting (and even instigating) more localized independence movements, as in Iran, Egypt, and India, where he urged militant cooper-ation by adherents of different faiths.

Ottoman maladministration and impotence, ac-centuated by constant imperialist pressure; Turk-ish predominance in Arab Asia; the despotism of ʿAbd ul-ḥamīd; the pride of the Arabs in their role in the creation and spread of Islam, as well as in the development of medieval Muslim civilization; and the flowering of Arabic literary studies (particularly in Christian circles in Beirut) all engendered hos-tility toward the Turks, which spread widely among Asian Arabs. Observers remarked this growing hostility in the 1880s. But discontent led to the idea of an Arab state (limited to Syria, Palestine, and Lebanon) only among a few Lebanese Christians around 1880. Separatism based on ethno-national identity was fostered by the independence movements of the Balkan Christian peoples, who sought freedom from the Ottoman Empire. But this only made the dissolution of that state, which invoked Islam as a sacred foundation, more repellent to Muslim Arabs.

The first unequivocal manifesto of modern Arab nationalism to have any influence was the work of 'Abd ar-raḥmān al-Kawākibī (1849–1903), a Syrian Muslim exile in Egypt. It was entitled *Umm al-qurā* (*The Mother of Cities*, i.e., Mecca) and appeared in 1901–2 at Cairo. The author extolled the superiority of the Arabs over the Turks and sketched a plan to regenerate Islam under the auspices of an Arab caliphate with uniquely spiritual powers, which was to be centered in the holy city of Mecca. He was strongly influenced by W. S. Blunt (1840–1922), a renowned British poet, anticolonialist, and ardent supporter of Egyptian independence and of the Arabs. In 1881 he gave vent to similar ideas in his book *The Future of Islam*. Kawākibī's ideas were taken up and developed by the Syro-Palestinian Christian Najīb 'Azūri (died 1916), who (along with a high-ranking French civil servant, Eugène Jung) founded a phantomlike "League of the Arab Fatherland" in Paris. 'Azūri published a book, *Le réveil de la nation arabe dans l'Asie turque* (Paris: Plon, 1905), and founded a review, *L'Indépendance arabe* (Paris, 1907–8). He was the first to propose an independent Arab empire. But the fact that he belonged to a minority group, that his propaganda was available only in France, and that he was probably involved with French colonial policy did much to militate against the success of his idea.

The First Organizations and the
Arab Revolt (1908–20)

The rebellion of the Young Turks (1908), which brought the Ottoman Empire a constitutional regime with a parliament, made it possible for all sorts of malcontents to organize. At the same time, the centralist policy followed by the Young Turks once they were in power and their increasing tendency to rely, despite their egalitarian pronouncements, on the Turkish segment of the populace increased discontentment in the Arab provinces. Organizations were set up to demand equal rights for Arabs within the Empire, local assemblies, and use of Arabic as an administrative, educational, and legal language in the Arabic-speaking regions. In particular, these demands constituted the program of the "Ottoman Party for Administrative Decentralization," founded in 1912. A reform committee was set up in Beirut. An Arab congress with Christian and Muslim delegates was held in Paris in 1912. Its demands were moderate and aimed mainly at the excessive centralization and Turkization of the regime. In the same period more radical secret societies were established, like the Qaḥṭāniya, which demanded an Arab-Turkish dual monarchy on the model of Austria-Hungary (1909); the Fatāt, which demanded Arab independence (1911); and *al-'Ahd*, which was composed primarily of Iraqi soldiers (1914).

When the Ottoman Empire went to war on the

side of Germany and Austria-Hungary (on November 2, 1914), more radical options were opened up. The sharīf of Mecca, Ḥusayn, and his sons were impelled by dynastic interest and hatred of the Young Turks to enter into relations with the Arab nationalists of the Fertile Crescent, who were organized in secret societies—some of them were in contact with France and Great Britian, which were looking to undermine the Ottoman enemy from within. When Jèmāl, the Turkish governor of Syria-Palestine, had Christian and Muslim Arab nationalists arrested for treason at Beirut and Damascus (in August 1915, April and May 1916), Sharīf Ḥusayn moved to open revolt. He proclaimed himself king of the Arabs (October 29, 1916), counting on promises that had been made to him in secret correspondence with Sir Henry MacMahon, the British High Commissioner in Egypt (July 1915-January 1916). England, France, and Italy recognized him only as king of the Hejāz. Ḥusayn's troops, organized by the English (most notably T. E. Lawrence), contributed to the defeat of the Turks. Damascus was taken on October 1, 1918.

The Allied victors did not honor the promises they had made to the Arabs to obtain their cooperation against the Turks. The Syrian General Congress proclaimed Fayṣal, son of Ḥusayn, constitutional king of Syria-Palestine (March 8, 1920). But General Gouraud drove him out of Damascus (July 25, 1920). Under the terms of the secret Sykes-Picot treaty (April-May 1916), the Arab countries of the Fertile Crescent were divided be-

tween France and Great Britain as League of Nations mandates. Syria and Lebanon became re-
publics (with fluctuating subdivisions) under
French mandate. Iraq was made a monarchy under
British mandate and Fayṣal was placed on the
throne. In accordance with Balfour's promise
(November 2, 1917), Palestine, under the mandate
and direct administration of the British, was split
off from Syria and opened up to Jewish colonization. East of the Jordan River, Transjordan was
split off from Palestine, and 'Abdullāh, Fayṣal's
brother, was allowed to reign there with the title of
emir, still under British mandate.

Struggles for Independence (1920–45)

The Arabs resented these measures as a betrayal
of the promises that had been made to them in
return for their agreement to aid the Allies. This
resentment produced paroxysms of frustration
and anger, which made the struggles for independence and unity of the following period particularly intense and which even today continue to
color Arab nationalist ideology.

After the great protest movements of the immediate postwar period for the application of Wil-
sonian principles of self-determination (the 1919
Egyptian insurrection against the English occupation) and against the betrayal of commitments
made to the Asian Arabs (riots in Palestine and a
major revolt in Iraq in 1920), there were few
genuine revolts, and those that did occur had local
causes: a Syrian insurrection (1925–27), a Palestinian peasant uprising (1936–39), the Rashīd 'Alī
Kaylāni movement in Iraq (April-May 1941). To

these movements, directly influenced or at least partially inspired by the nationalist ideas of the eastern Arabs, we must add the isolated rebellion of Abd el-Krim in the Moroccan Rif (1921–26), which, though confined to the immediate area, made its echoes heard far away. Popular discontent in the Near East made itself felt in a virtually uninterrupted series of strikes, demonstrations, and riots, which were followed and inevitably strengthened by repressive measures.

Though Great Britian and France did resort to repression, they also moved from time to time to allay the hunger for new rights. The eastern states (with the exception of Palestine) were granted formal independence in treaties with the European power involved. But these treaties themselves were the cause of protest. The source of trouble lay in the prerogatives they reserved to the European powers. The Arab leaders (monarchs in the countries under English influence, republican officials in those under French mandate) hesitated or wavered between "collaboration" and protest.

The masses longed for independence without any prompting; they were hostile to the colonial powers, and showed contempt and hatred for the native rulers who were all too ready to "collaborate." But these deep-seated hopes and feelings, which grew out of the situation, had hardly begun to be laid out explicitly in the form of an ideology. The major worldwide ideologies also made their influence felt. Liberalism, a source of inspiration for the preceding period, was on the wane. Communist Marxism popularized the idea of independence coupled with the antiimperialist struggle and attracted some sympathy in the period 1920–22, but its influence was quite limited. Fascist ideology, promoted by a powerful propaganda, aroused some sympathy in the East after 1933. The attraction lay in its nationalist foundation and in its identification of the enemies: Great Britain, France, the Jews.

The idea of Arab unity, first conceived in Arab Asia in opposition to the fragmentation enforced by the authorities, began to attract supporters in Africa. It should be noted that in its broad form, encompassing all Arab countries, it was first formulated around 1930 by the tiny communist parties of the Arab countries, which formed a bloc within the Third International. At best this ideology could have exerted only a limited and indirect influence, since these parties represented tiny, clandestine minorities and hardly anyone was aware of their publications. Little by little, though, the unity idea took hold: it was a product of the situation and not of this communist literature, which reflected reality in its own fashion, tinged by the class struggle. In situations where the struggle for independence is paramount and national unity takes precedence, emphasis on class struggle is not likely to attract supporters.

Arabist ideology spread first into Egypt. There, a powerful Egyptian nationalist movement (whose slogan was "Egypt for the Egyptians") had grown up in the struggle against British rule, though this did not mean that the feeling of being part of the Arab ethnos was repudiated (or emphasized). Beginning in 1936 the need for some kind of unity with other Arab peoples became apparent to many

Egyptians. The predominant role of the Egyptian press and radio and of Egyptian music, film, and publishing throughout the Egyptian world, which was aided by expanded educational opportunities and technological progress, gave added significance to this development.

There were, of course, centrifugal tendencies: economic special interests and a new local patriotism in the recently created states (alongside the thousand-year-old Egyptian nationalism); the "realistic" attitudes of many government officials; ideologies based on the pre-Islamic and pre-Arab past in certain countries (limited to a few intellectuals); strength of communal religious feelings (particularly in Lebanon); a Fascist-leaning ideology based on the geographical unity of "Greater Syria," which was developed by the Syrian Popular Party (founded in 1933); and so on. But the ideology of unity was paramount.

After the Second World War broke out in 1939, Arab opinion adopted a wait-and-see attitude, with some sympathies for the Axis engendered by hostility toward Great Britain and France. To win back the good graces of the Arabs, the English put a stop to Jewish immigration into Palestine (May 1939 White Paper), declared themselves in sympathy with Arab unity (Eden declaration of May 29, 1941), and helped the states of the Levant win total independence from Free France (Lebanon in 1943, Syria in 1945). These measures culminated in the constitution of the League of Arab States, whose charter was signed in Cairo (March 22, 1945) under British auspices. At last there was a supranational political structure embodying the idea of

Arab unity. As yet this included only states that had
won at least formal independence in Arabia (Saudi
Arabia and Yemen) and the Fertile Crescent (Iraq,
Syria, Lebanon, Transjordan), along with Egypt.

From the Arab League to the
United Arabic Republic (1945–58)

The Arab League was far from satisfying the
ideological aspirations of the Arab peoples. It did,
of course, play a useful role in the areas of culture,
economics, and administration. But it did not suc-
ceed in formulating a common policy. Even when
policy outlooks were identical, there was more
coordination of propaganda than of concrete action. Opposite tendencies confronted one another
within the League on the most crucial questions,
sometimes reaching the point of open hostility.
Last but not least, British influence, in evidence
from the very beginning of the League, continued
for some time to be a potent force, leading to
doubts of the League's independence.

The Arab peoples were disappointed by the
landed aristocracy, which until then had led the
movement and which they suspected, not without
reason, of self-regarding conservatism and collusion with foreign imperialists. They demanded a
more strenuous policy against the French (for
independence of the Arab Maghrib), the British
(who had held on to their protectorates in Arabia
and the Sudan and to strong positions in Egypt and
Iraq), and the new state of Israel, which was
established in 1948 at the cost of dividing an Arab
territory and which in that same year inflicted a

crushing defeat on the disorganized and badly-led Arab forces. This defeat aggravated the old frustrations and injuries. It is still painfully remembered by the hundreds of thousands of dispossessed Palestinians driven into exile as a consequence.

Hostility toward the Western powers (and the upper strata of the society seemingly in league with them) grew as a result of efforts by the colonizers to enlist Arab support in the Cold War and to form a chain of allies by means of military agreements with the countries lying to the south of the Soviet Union. Arab nationalists, who saw no threat from the Soviets, viewed these efforts with extreme suspicion, even in anticommunist quarters. Arab sentiment was focused on decolonization and reconquest of the occupied territories (eastern and southern Arabia, the Maghrib, Israel, etc.), removal of the remaining fetters on complete autonomy for the already independent countries (military bases, treaty provisions allowing return of British troops under certain circumstances, etc.), and internal reform through exclusion from political life of the pro-Western upper classes, who were held responsible for past defeats. In the eyes of the nationalists the alliance with the West was a ruse for maintaining the status quo, increasing imperialist intervention, and perpetuating the power of the ruling classes. American efforts to use broad Islamic groupings as a device for turning Arab hostility against atheistic communism were eyed warily. These went hand in hand on the political side with pressure to form alliances with the Turks, who

were not fondly remembered by the Arabs; with
the Iranians, who were held in low esteem; and,
implicitly, even with Israel. Like Germany in years
past, the U.S.S.R. now appeared, whether rightly
or wrongly, to be the great noncolonialist power,
the enemy of the enemies of the Arabs.

Such feelings were the root cause of unrest in
Syria, where public opinion took on a neutralist
cast during a period marked by a series of military
coups d'état (after 1949). In September 1954, the left,
in the form of the Ba'th party (the socialist party of
the Arab renaissance), won the Syrian elections. A
communist took office. The Egyptian revolution
(July 23, 1952) brought to power a nationalist
group (headed by Nasser) which at first sought to
maintain a pro-Western orientation. The Baghdad
pact (February-April 1955), which linked Turkey,
Iraq, Iran, and Pakistan under the aegis of the
United States and Britain, impelled the Egyptian
officers, who were hostile to Turkish and Iraqi
leadership, to turn gradually toward an alliance
with the socialist bloc. Nasser met with Chou En-lai
at Bandung (April 1955) and purchased arms from
Czechoslovakia (September 1955). The American
refusal to finance the Aswan dam provoked the
Egyptians to nationalize the Suez Canal (July 1956).
The intervention of the English, French, and Israelis at Suez (October-November 1956), which
failed because of the reaction of the Russians and
the Americans, further radicalized Arab nationalist
sentiment.

The radical turn was also heightened by the

Algerian uprising (November 1954) and the independence of the Sudan (1955), Tunisia, and Morocco (1956). The United States lost what popularity it had gained by its attitude during the Suez campaign: the Eisenhower doctrine (January 1957) allowed for intervention by American troops if called for by a country "threatened by international communism." The uncompromising hostility of the Americans toward the neutralist regime in Syria and the fear on the part of the Ba'th of rising communist power there led that party to urge Nasser, the leader of the Egyptian officers, whose popularity as an "Arab national hero" had grown immense after Suez, to form a union between Syria and Egypt. After much hesitation Nasser proclaimed the establishment of the United Arab Republic (February 1, 1958), which included (theoretically, at least) Yemen. The enthusiasm of the Arab world for this development is indescribable; Arabs looked upon the event as the laying of the cornerstone of a great Arab union, for which they had long been yearning.

Theoreticians and Theories

After the pioneers of antiimperialist protonationalism, who dreamed of freedom and reform within the context of the Ottoman Empire and the Muslim community, it took a long time for Arab nationalism to find its theoreticians. Without prompting, men working toward independence by trying to mobilize the widespread but scarcely conscious feelings of the masses tended to concentrate their efforts on the Asian Arabs. The question of extending the movement to African Arabs was considered only sporadically and always in a hesitant and indecisive way, if not rejected out of hand. The first nationalists in the Maghrib focused their efforts on winning the right to make independent decisions. In North Africa (in contrast to the Near East), to belong to the Muslim community was to be aware of being Arab—even speakers of Berber were attracted by Arab ideals. Accordingly, apart from local demands appeal was made only to a vague amalgam of Arab and Muslim solidarity. Here and there embryonic theories appeared in the utterances of journalists and politicians, in speeches, tracts, newspaper articles, and reviews.

Mention was made earlier (p. 97) of the theories of the communists of the 1930s, theories which were in fact pan-Arabist and which remained virtually unread. One of the earliest theoreticians to attract an audience was Edmond Rabbath, a Christian from Aleppo, whose book *Unité syrienne et devenir arabe* (Paris: Rivère, 1937) was written in French. He was followed by two Lebanese writers, the Christian Constantin Zurayq (beginning in 1938) and the Muslim ʿAbdullāh al-ʿAlāyilī (1941); by the Syrian Muslim Ṣātiʿal-Ḥuṣrī, a former Ottoman and Iraqi official, who wrote many books on this theme during the 1940s and later; and by many others.

Arab nationalism has fashioned for itself an ideology which includes a theory of the nation and in particular of the Arab nation—a theory put together in response to the spontaneous aspirations and practical political problems arising out of the experience of the Arab peoples, but using ideological tools fabricated in Europe. From European theories of the nation the Arabs borrowed the idea of defending and extolling a common language and history, on which they have placed greater stress than on territorial ties. Arab theoreticians have laid down a unifying foundation for the Arab nation, which is considered a *qawmiya* (from *qawm*, "people," modeled on *Volkstum*), whereas the tendency has been to exclude or minimize the importance of the concept of *waṭaniya* (from *waṭan*, "place of birth or residence, fatherland," in which the territorial factor is essential), meaning "patriotism." Regional patriotism based on the distinctive characteristics of the various Arab states has been played down, being designated by pejorative terms such as *iqlīmiya*, "regionalism." Such local feelings were impediments to solidarity in countries whose frontiers had only recently been established, often by the European powers, and which in most cases lacked the power to arouse strong feelings of allegiance. Even in Egypt, where a powerful local national sentiment has existed since antiquity, early theoretical attempts to formulate an Egyptian nationalism were obliged to give precedence, at least outwardly, to Arab nationalism.

What was evolved was a kind of "sacred history," which exalts the great deeds of the Arab people in the past and blames all untoward occurrences on Turkish, Iranian, or European influence. Quite often all the great achievements of the Semitic-speaking peoples prior to the Arab expansion are credited to Arabism; Berbers, Egyptians, and Copts are considered to have been Arabs ever since the days of antiquity. The ideas and values of modern Arab nationalism have been read back into the Arab past. All history has been directed toward one goal: the establishment (deemed a reestablishment) of a strong, unified Arab nation.

From this teleology an ethical code has been derived. In keeping with the romantic tradition of Fichte and Hegel, the individual is subordinated to the nation, in a manner that also harks back to premodern social conceptions. The individual's duty is to sacrifice himself for the nation, and, if need be, he must be compelled to do so. The nation is the supreme value, and this supremacy is justified by an argument along secular lines. But traditional notions of submission to the state or the religious community (Islam) have been reinterpreted and put to use from this new standpoint.

Islam has been interpreted less as a divine revelation about mankind, the world, and God than as an Arab national value. Even Christian Arabs recognize it as such and exalt the role of Mohammed, unifier of the Arabs and initiator of their expansion. Moderate versions of Arabism make room for "regional" allegiances (which account for a two-tier variety of nationalism), the rights of ethnic minorities, and particular observances of religious minorities. But extremist versions have been very influential, particularly during crises. Past collusion of minorities with the European powers, their present role as agents of European capitalist penetration of the East, and the external loyalties implied by all this—for example, the dependence of the

Christian churches on foreign authorities—have sometimes been used to arouse suspicion of them. This suspicion (via a vicious circle that impels the injured minority groups to look elsewhere for support, justifying suspicion *a posteriori*) may lead (at certain times in certain countries) to discrimination in the award of official posts against minorities and in favor of Muslim Arabs (sometimes, still more exclusively, of Sunnite Arabs). All other things being equal, there is a vague feeling that the nationalism of the right kind of Muslim is more trustworthy.

In general, Arab nationalism has to some degree at least had revolutionary overtones, because the need was to strike at established conditions and the social strata that profited from them through their ties with the Western economies. Nationalism developed in the bosom of the middle class but has exerted a strong influence on other classes. This nationalism has never managed to acquire a unified organization and unified political leadership, but the sentiments and aspirations that underlie it have been powerful enough to permit spontaneous though sometimes transitory mass mobilizations in behalf of its immediate objectives and ideals, as well as to compel conservatives to acquiesce in certain of its aims. The conservatives have had to deal cautiously with the movement and have largely limited their efforts to slowing it down and steering it away from extremist goals intolerable to them.

In some cases the pattern of political forces in the world, in others pressure from disadvantaged social strata, have influenced the elaboration of

ideologies that try to reconcile Arab nationalism
with the ideal of a just society. Even before the
Second World War, Arab communists had made
efforts in this direction. After the war, the Baʻth
party tried to set forth a theory of Arab socialism.
At first the accent was on the nationalist element,
but a Baʻthist left wing attempted to place more
stress on the socialist ideal. Later, nationalization
measures forced on the Egyptian government by
internal and external conditions that posed a threat
to its objectives of independence and modernization (as well as the support those objectives received
from the socialist bloc) led to the elaboration of an
"Arab socialism" (Nasserism). Conflicts between
states and organizations championing one or
another of these various tendencies led to some
efforts to extend the associated theories, but a relatively simple form of nationalism has continued to
predominate. Arab Marxists have tried to shore up
the theoretical foundations of the socialist compo-
nent of nationalist ideology, but their efforts still bear
a Stalinist stamp, even when they are made outside
the ranks of the communist parties *per se*. The
ideas, attitudes, and practical prescriptions of the
Marxists have, however, had a much wider influence and have spawned several varieties of
nationalism with more or less pronounced Marxist
leanings.

Practical Theories in Action

Some of these theories were worked out by individual intellectuals interested in making a contri-
bution to their people's struggles. Their ideas were

not without repercussions. As we have seen, these ideas were in some cases designed to provide a theoretical foundation for a party engaged in political conflict (such as the Ba'th party), while in other cases they were conceived after a party or group had seized power, at which point the simple guiding principles that had served until then needed to be extended and elaborated (as with Nasserism). The influence of theories backed by groups in power, or at any rate by political organizations, has been considerable, incomparably greater than the influence of the pure intellectuals. By influencing attention-getting political activity, these theories helped to mold attitudes and shape collective ideas and feelings.

The aspirations of the masses, whose significant features, taken together, formed the outlines of a vague ideology, were thus gathered up in party ideologies and further focused, sharpened, and spelled out in detail. These ideas then exerted an influence on the programs and policies of governments, which in turn affected the thinking of the masses. Before ideology could be embodied in a program, of course, governments first had to interpret its content according to their own lights.

By such a process, Arabism, an amalgam of quite vague, general tendencies, aspirations, and ideas, was bodied forth in several mass ideologies, one of which held sway for a period of fifteen years, mainly in the Arab East, though it was not without influence in the Maghrib as well. I am speaking, of course, of Nasserism, an ideology inextricably intertwined with the personality of a prestigious, charismatic leader whose spectacular doings had won the affection of the masses and brought him to power in the most populous, as well as in several ways the strongest and most influential, country in the Arab world: Egypt. This man was Gamāl 'Abd an-Nāser (Nasser).

Dominance of Nasserism (1958–70)

Between 1958 and 1970, then, the Arab masses were mainly subject to the influence of Arabist ideology in its Nasserist form, challenges and countercurrents of several kinds notwithstanding. Again, this was a form of Arab nationalism that emphasized the desirability of unifying the entire Arab nation. The principal enemy was "imperialism," a term used exclusively to refer to the economic and political policies by which the Western capitalist powers, above all the United States, ensured their hegemony. Though indeed a real influence, "imperialism" was mythified, conceived as emanating from a single source, a sort of monstrous, evil personality whose tentacles reached into every corner and out of which hatched an endless series of Machiavellian plots aimed at the freedom and prosperity of other nations, and particularly at Arab unification. The form of social organization appropriate to the Arab nation was held to be "Arab socialism," i.e., a state capitalism that would protect a developing autonomy from the threat of surbordination to the liberal economy, a threat that was only the more dangerous for being surreptitious. Implicit in this state function were economic planning and authoritarian control, whereas the name—socialism—by which these activities were called suggested to the masses a natural hostility to inequality and privilege. Islam was respected, thanks to an interpretation that saw it as consistent with the requirements of "socialism" and Arabism, though no interference by the clergy in the running of the state was tolerated. The archaic provisions of traditional Islamic law were made more flexible and modern by way of indulgent exegesis. Alliance with the communist states was sought as an indispensable counterweight to the hostility of the West, but their ideology and their local spokesmen were eyed warily, was were local communists and other Marxists. A wary eye was also cast on any suggestion that the class struggle might be continuing within the "Arab socialist" state, that Arabism and Islam might not be sufficient guarantees against exploitation and oppression and might even serve to camouflage them.

The Western public by and large looked upon Nasserism as a corrupt and pernicious ideology, a noxious, imperalistic "pan-Arabism" that awakened bad memories of pan-Germanism. Westerners failed to understand that the slogan of Arab unity, no less than the claim to Palestine, was indispensable to any leader whose aim was to secure a mass base for his power. In practical terms, moreover, Nasser's policy in these two areas was in fact quite moderate, however ardent his public pronouncements may have been. He was drawn into the disastrous June 1967 war by his own initiatives, imposed on him by his role as a popular ruler; he failed to see both the full extent of the implications of the move and the strength of the Israeli reaction that it would trigger, and though aware of the relative weakness of his own army, he failed to comprehend the depth of its inadequacy. The wealthy classes in Egypt held against him the measures of nationalization that were necessary if the ailing Egyptian economy was to be steered toward independence. The dictatorial and police-state measures, which were rightly denounced by their victims on both right and left, were the local version (carried out with particular brutality and stupidity) of the usual forms of coercion practiced by regimes of this type.

Nationalist ideology invariably presents itself as inspired solely by the interests and aspirations of the entire nation. It is nonetheless marked with the undeniable stamp of the class or classes responsible for shaping and diffusing it, and it is nonetheless expressive of their particular interests. In Egypt, Nasserism was the expression of the interests of the middle strata, whose feelings were sincerely nationalist and antiimperalist but more than willing to accept state control of the economy and a larger state-run sector. Though aware of the necessity to modernize the society, the middle classes were nevertheless primarily concerned to avoid serious social upheaval and were afraid of the uncouth underclasses. The tremendous expansion of the state sector provided jobs and stipends (in military and civilian sectors alike) for a broad new class, which established close ties with the vestiges of the deposed ruling class: the landowners and wealthy bourgeois. Many of these former rulers were integrated into the new system. Both inside and outside Egypt, this new class adopted a policy of prudent compromise and carefully controlled initiative; in the eyes of the masses, however, this policy was still enveloped in the aura of prestige that surrounded the leader.

Nasserism's major competitor in the East was Ba'thism, whose class base and general orientation were practically the same. But the Ba'th leaders never managed to acquire Nasser's prestige, and their power base in Syria and Iraq did not afford them the same springboard for spectacular ventures.

None of the considerable hopes the masses placed in this leadership and ideology was realized. The union of Syria and Egypt under the name United Arab Republic (February 1958), soon complemented by a loose federation (potentially open to other members) with Yemen (March 8) known as the United Arab States, quickly proved a disappointment to the ideologues who had been led to believe that the creation of a unified Arab state was at last in sight, and that the unification of the Arab lands must now proceed at an accelerating pace.

The ties with Yemen, one of the most archaic of nations, at that time ruled by a patriarchal despot, were never made concrete. The economic interests of the Syrians and the activities of their political groups were infringed upon by the authoritarianism of the Egyptian offiicials and military, who looked upon the "northern region" of the U.A.R. as subordinate to Egypt. This led to Syria's secession from the union (September 28, 1961).

The ideal of union survived in the several state constitutions in which it was officially inscribed, in the title "United Arab Republic" long retained by Egypt, in that of "Syrian Arab Republic" adopted by Syria, and in similar names chosen by other countries. The Arab states have since adopted widely divergent policies within the framework of their League, and a good many more or less temporary coalitions have been put together, frequently in direct rivalry with one another, only to dissolve after short period. Morocco, for example, went so far as to challenge the independence of Mauritania, and a war lasting a few days broke out in October 1963 between Algeria and Morocco. There was a threat of its being rekindled in February 1976 over the issue of the former Spanish Sahara. At the time of this writing, instead of a direct war the "Frente Polisario," whose program is based on autonomy for this region, is with Algerian support conducting an active guerrilla campaign against Morocco and Mauritania, which have divided the area between themselves. In polemic, Algeria and especially Morocco have spoken of historic rights and tried to stir up "regional" nationalism, which is logically in contradiction with the broader Arab nationalism. Other conflicts between Arab countries, though not carried to quite such lengths, have often taken a bitter turn.

Arab countries forced to fight major battles have often failed to win the support of other Arab countries. Only a few overriding common causes have been able to bring all Arab nations together, but only briefly (and never wholeheartedly): these include support for Arab nations still fighting for independence from colonial powers (Kuwait, 1961; Algeria, 1962; South Yemen, 1967; the emirates of the Persian Gulf, 1971) and the struggle over the last occupied territory, Israel (June 1967 and October 1973 wars).

Left-wing Arabism against Right-wing Arabism

Both Nasserism and Ba'thism failed to achieve Arab unity and to resolve the problem of Israel and the Palestinians. Nowhere was economic performance brilliant, and Nasser's Egypt in particular sank into destitution and cultural decline. The new classes in power were often painfully reminiscent of the old. The June 1967 fiasco raised the question of the adequacy of old ideas for solving the pressing problems of the day.

Every major problem, every failure, every crisis that arose in pursuit of the ideal of Arab nationalism led to feelings that something was lacking in nationalist ideology, that other important ideologies should be looked to as sources of fresh ideas. The assumption was that failure, crisis, and disillusionment could be explained by the fact that the newly discovered element had previously been overlooked. The new ideas were imported by new generations or social strata, who blamed failure on the complacency of their predecessors in their acquired status and saw opportunities for themselves in taking charge of the movement.

The first communist offensive of the 1920s and its renewal in the Levant after 1936 and again in 1944 were efforts to reinterpret Arab nationalism in a Marxist framework. The founding of the Ba'th party in 1943 was an attempt to give Arab nationalism a "socialist" sense with the fewest possible communist connotations. But as with Nasserism, experience in power showed up the limitations of "socialism" so conceived and led to disappointment for the banal reason that what was achieved was a long way indeed from what had originally been hoped for.

In about 1960 new and still unformed movements began to appear with the goal of steering the national struggles on a more radical course and hence of explaining the supposed laxity of the existing leadership. The groups influenced by these views found an attractive international model of radical, revolutionary struggle in the broad range of extreme left-wing groups (the "New Left" in the English-speaking countries, the "gauchistes" in France). The ideology that was supposed to invigorate this political line (given an added fillip by Chinese-inspired theory with a special aura attached to the Third World and Asia) was baptized "Marxism-Leninism," though frequently the demand for some sort of revolution was the only (or virtually the only) common ground between these groups and the ideas of Marx and Lenin.

Thus, in the Movement of Arab Nationalists (*al-qawmiyūn al-'Arab*), an initially clandestine Beirut youth group boasting a high proportion of Palestinians among its members and proclaiming nationalist objectives, which for a time was enthusiastically Nasserist, a clear left wing emerged in 1964. Criticism of the government's cautious policies led little by little to denunciation not only of the old ruling classes but also of the Nasserite and Ba'thist bureaucracy, whose vices were seemingly made manifest by the 1967 defeat.[1]

Events in southern Arabia played a large part in all these developments. For many people Nasserism was discredited by the hegemonic ambitions and high-handedness it displayed in North Yemen, where the Egyptians intervened military in support of the Yemeni republicans (1962–67). In the struggle against the British in South Yemen, the Nasserite FLOSY (Front for the Liberation of Occupated South Yemen) was all too ready to act as an agent of Cairo's strategy. The Arabian branches of the Arab Nationalist Movement (ANM, established in the 1950s), initially Nasserite, broke their Nasserite ties and adopted a "Marxist-Leninist" orientation. Defeated in North Yemen, this left wing came to power in South Yemen in 1969. For the Palestinians, too, Nasserite domination became increasingly intolerable. The revolt against Nasserism, the desire to take an independent tack, and the tendency to seek the causes of the defeat in "betrayal" by Arab rulers were also colored by "Marxism-Leninism." A Marxist-leaning Ba'thist left held power in Syria from 1966 to 1970.

Only in the Maghrib (in Algeria and Morocco) did the old-line communists continue to represent the bulk of the Marxist left, though increasingly they were forced underground. To date, ultrarevolutionary "leftism" in the Maghrib has attracted only a few tiny and uninfluential groups.

1. Concerning the Arab Nationalist Movement and the Arabian movements, see the excellent book by Fred Halliday, *Arabia without Sultans* (Harmondsworth: Pelican Books, 1974).

Criticism from the left by Algerian and Moroccan communists is respectful of the powers-that-be: the FLN (National Liberation Front) in Algeria and King Hassan II in Morocco.

In opposition to these various leftist movements, a rightist reaction has taken shape in recent years and by the force of events acquired considerable influence. This rehabilitation began with the defeat of Nasser by Israel in June 1967. Egyptian economic distress after the loss of the Sinai and the closing of the Suez canal, coupled with Nasserism's declining prestige, gave the upper hand to King Faisal of Saudi Arabia (assassinated in March 1975), a Muslim fundamentalist, prudent modernizer, and fierce opponent of all social change. With the emirs of the Persian Gulf, he exercised considerable power thanks to the enormous revenues derived from petroleum. This enabled him to impose conditions in return for his economic assistance to the Arab states, which particularly in the East was urgently required. The crushing defeat of the Palestinians in Jordan during the "Black September" of 1970, followed immediately by the death of Nasser, only enhanced Saudi dominance. In Egypt, Nasser's successor, Anwar as-Sādāt, revamped what remained of Nasser's "socialist" programs. In Syria, too, the ultrarevolutionaries were deposed in November 1970. The direct influence of the Saudis lies behind North Yemen's return to a nonrevolutionary course in 1968. And even South Yemen was in the end (1976) compelled by its poverty and political isolation to moderate its revolutionary plans and seek a *modus vivendi* with Saudi Arabia.

This move to the right was bolstered by its successes: the October 1973 war in which for the first time an Arab state won substantial military victories against Israel, the September 1975 interim agreement by Israel to evacuate part of the Sinai, and above all the increase in the financial power of Arab petroleum states owing to the price hikes decreed by OPEC. The spectacular restoration of American economic power after a brief period of apparent decline tends in the same direction.

The Build-up of Arab Power

These successes put into the hands of the monarchs of the Arabian peninsula the means to press other Arab states to support their policies. At stake was the creation of an Arab bloc, which by avoiding the prestige and the pitfalls of formal political unification might achieve power on the world scene. Practical unity, it was hoped, would emerge from an alliance between the ruling strata of the despotic states, whose princes had investments in finance, commerce, and industry, and the new classes holding power in the countries with state capitalist economies.

The considerable extent of the financial power wielded by this new bloc—whose political independence is now undisputed—should enable it to play a world role in alliance with the United States, a choice of ally dictated as much by the conservatism of the peninsula's rulers as by a dispassionate analysis of the balance of power. Its financial power should also enable this bloc to keep from becoming an American satellite and to obtain in return for its cooperation a share in the profits of American

hegemony. It might be possible to make room for
the American protectorate Israel, however little the
Jewish state cares to allow it; this would be done by
returning Israel to its 1967 borders, as a way of
disarming the revolutionary opposition engendered by the Palestinian situation, which might
otherwise mobilize the Arab masses in a challenge to
the status quo. Patient pressure on the Americans
(whose difficulties are readily comprehensible) has
been designed to push them into obtaining the
necessary concessions from Israel.

In practice the Saudi plan has by and large won
the assent and cooperation even of regimes that
maintain socialist-leaning policies and ties with the
Soviet Union: Iraq, Syria, Algeria. Though Syria
has expanded the private sector, these states have
not abandoned the idea of making the state
capitalist sector the cutting edge of economic development, nor have they ceased to spread a fairly
egalitarian ideology and to take actions that indicate little sympathy with the policies of the
United States. They maintain cautious relations
with the American-dominated world capitalist system, hoping to rake in the profits without becoming bogged down in the hidden dependencies
engendered by this mode of production and tar-
nishing their reputations as revolutionaries. But
practical (though hestitant and covert) participa-
tion in the new Arab bloc is for the moment (1978)
the basic course these states have chosen.

In decades past the general orientation of
Arabism made it possible to align the struggle for
its victory with the aims of the left throughout the

world. For many Arabs, disillusioned by the solidity of the conservative regimes and the direction taken by the revolutionary ones, this identification with left-wing ideology has been broken. At present the triumph of Arabism seems instead to depend on financial, technological, and military power which operates independently but is tied to the capitalist world. Nationalism persists but for many has taken on a conservative coloration. Stabilization is therefore the order of the day. The authorities accordingly lend their support to ideologies that appeal to national cohesiveness, with their exaltation of identity and "authenticity," including fidelity to Islamic identity. A fair proportion of the masses, disillusioned by ideologies of revolutionary change, has also turned in this direction. Many take refuge in pietistic and mystical moralism. The clergy, on the whole conservative, encourages this response in those who turn to it for counsel.

The Algerian authorities, though they do enforce to some degree the puritanism preached by the clergy, have adopted a cautious attitude and limit clerical activities to a carefully circumscribed area. The two antagonistic factions of the Ba'th party, which theoretically hold power in Syria and Iraq, have tried to preserve the party's original secular outlook. Nowhere is clerical rule desired as a goal.

The wealthy and conservative governments of Arabia exert considerable pressure on other states, many of them partially dependent on their subsidies, to win support for their policies. They are especially concerned to bring about a complete

break with the Soviet Union. Despite the Soviets'
"good behavior," their rivalry with the United
States and the color of their official ideology, which
still has some effect abroad, have often led to
alliances with "destabilizing" movements, at least in
the Third World. Tunisia, Mauritania, and
Morocco were predisposed to such an arrange-
ment, though the influence of potentially profitable
trade agreements with Moscow is not to be dis-
counted. Egypt and Morocco once lent their support to the Russians. In North Yemen, Ḥamdī, the
supreme leader, who had shown a willingness to
effect reconciliation with Marxist South Yemen
and a concern to throw off the yoke of tribal
chieftains financed by Saudi Arabia, was conve-
niently assassinated (October 11, 1977) in rather
murky circumstances.

The Saudis moved to co-opt and reorient the
policies of several Arab states on the Red Sea and
the horn of Africa. Against the Ethiopian empire,
dominated by the pro-American and pro-Israeli
Christian Amharas, these states had been aiding
both the Eritrean guerrillas and socialist Muslim
Somalia, a Soviet ally, which was accepted as a
member of the Arab League in February 1974 despite the small proportion of Arabs in its population. The Saudi move was either set off or speeded
up by events following the fall of emperor Haile
Selassie (September 1974), by the establishment of
a revolutionary regime in Ethiopia, and above all
by the Soviet choice of that country as its African
bastion and ally (in February 1977 or thereabouts).
Significantly, most of the "progressive" Arab

countries joined the conservative states in continuing to aid both the Eritrean guerrillas, whose
ideological allegiances were divided, and Somalia,
which, though socialist, now turned to the West for
support.

The new bloc has, however, met with opposition
or quasi opposition within the Arab world. For one
thing, South Yemen, faithful to its alliance with the
Soviets, has given aid to Ethiopia. For another,
neither the Palestinians nor Libya has fallen into
line.

The Libyan case is rather paradoxical. By all indications the young officers and their charismatic
leader, Colonel Qaddāfi, who came to power in a
September 1, 1969 putsch, should have been in-
clined to follow the line of the new bloc. Qaddāfi
has from the outset shown a fierce disdain for
atheist Marxism, the Soviet Union, and the class
struggle. He has exhibited an Islamic fundamen-
talism unmatched outside Saudi Arabia. But at the
same time he has remained sincerely and often in-
genuously attached to the leading values of the two
other ideologies of the Arab world, nationalism
and socialism, with sometimes curious consequences. Qaddāfi has elaborated and attempted to
put into practice a theory (set forth in "green
books") that claims to resolve all political, economic, and social problems through a socialist-
leaning Islam. Libya has been transformed from a
jumhūrīya (republic) to a *jamāhīrīya* (state of the
masses). A vigilant antiimperialism, accentuated by
the revelation of hidden dependence on the world
capitalist system, by American support for Israel,

and by the compromises struck by Sadat's Egypt and the Sudan, has impelled Libya to seek the support of the Soviet Union, once spurned but, in the final analysis, the only available source of aid.

The new bloc is much embarrassed by the problem of the Palestinians, whose claims it cannot repudiate. It supports the centrist group that formally heads up the PLO, a very loose coalition of heterogeneous organizations. This center group is ready to settle for far less than what it had originally demanded, to accept coexistence with an Israel cut down more or less to its pre-1967 borders. But it has had a very difficult time convincing its mass base of support to accept this solution, so difficult that it has not as yet dared make a clear proposal to that effect. This vacillation, together with the excesses of the extremist groups, has contributed to Israeli intransigence and American hesitancy on the issue. This in turn has created a vicious circle by increasing the difficulties the Palestinian centrists face in winning acceptance for their views and stating them openly and clearly.

The embarrassment reached its height with the spectacular initiative taken in November 1977 by Egyptian President Sadat, which was motivated by the disastrous economic situation in Egypt and fear of dangerous social movements. The strength of Egyptian national feeling could have lent mass support to his quest for a quick peace. But he seemed to go too far, too fast, in according full, indeed warm, recognition to the Jewish state, with nothing certain gained in return. The refusal of

Israel, led by Mr. Begin's ultranationalist government since May 1977, to offer any concessions impelled the Arab states most favorably disposed toward Sadat's initiative, as well as the PLO leadership after brief hesitation, to issue a blunt rejection
of the move. After pressure from the Americans
had forced Begin to make concessions, postponed
for the most part until later, Sadat was able to go
further toward concluding a separate peace with
Israel at Camp David in September 1978; a
framework agreement outlining the shape of an
overall settlement lent legitimacy to his participa-
tion.

In reaction to the November 1977 initiative, a
motley coalition established a so-called hard-line
front (thereby avoiding the name first favored by
the group, rejection front), which brought into the
open a split in the newly forming bloc. The Camp
David agreements helped somewhat to consolidate
this coalition. It is a heterogeneous grouping, however, which does not augur well for its durability.
Their public pronouncements notwithstanding,
some of its members are hardly willing to abandon
the alliance with the United States. The Soviets
have offered their support and the future may see
a further willingness to accept Soviet aid, but this
may well cause new problems and lead to drastic
changes in the situation. There is a potential breach
hidden in the conflict between those who would
like to see a compromise peace concluded on better
terms (different from one country to the next) than
Sadat obtained (this is Moscow's viewpoint), and

the proponents (whether sincere or not) of all-out revolutionary war. Many hesitate to choose between the alternatives.

It is difficult in any case to imagine Saudi Arabia (along with the Gulf states and Jordan) giving up the heart of its plan and the means for making it work out of love for the Palestinians. All that Saudi Arabia wants is for the Americans to pressure Israel into making concessions more plausible to Arab public opinion. Only a revolution in Riyadh could change this stand.

As things stand at present, none of the aspirations of recent decades has been fulfilled. Throughout large segments of the society, rebellious attitudes toward old and new bourgeoisies persist, along with suspicion, to put it mildly, of the capitalist world that apparently props them up. These attitudes are constantly revitalized by social dissatisfaction and the enduring wound of Palestine. They grow in strength to the extent that the conservative regimes have shown themselves incapable of healing that wound, and as Israeli intransigence and American indulgence of Israel on the issue become increasingly evident.

Certain of the present regimes and their ideologues, whether sincerely or cynically, are in fact attempting to use the incipient violence of the dissatisfied for their own purposes, to put the revolutionary spirit to work in building a new center of power in the world. This violence has been interpreted as on ongoing revolution against the capitalist world or industrial society, a revenge against Europe by an advance guard of pariah peoples of the Third World. This rather incoherent, syncretistic ideology has met with some success. But at the same time exploited groups in the new system are taking this doctrine's revolutionary tenets seriously, and this tendency spells danger for the system.

America and Europe worry both about the build-up of Arab power as a possible future competitor, a competitor already in possession of commanding financial wherewithal, and about the prospect of revolution. Arabism's revolutionary image persists because of the enduring memory of spectacular acts of defiance in the recent past, because of the pressures withstood in the hope of obtaining greater concessions, the continued hostility toward Israel, the terrorist methods used by elements of the Palestinian movement and their allies, the sporadic explosions of the wretched Arab masses, the presence of large numbers of Arab sub-proletarians in the industrial world, and, lastly, because of alliances or threats of alliance with the U.S.S.R. For Europeans and Americans Islam bears the stigma—which for the Third World is a mark of prestige—of having been the implacable enemy of a Christianity linked to European culture. The 1978–79 Islamic revolution in Iran can only have strengthened this opinion.

This accounts for the sometimes unexpected support that has been given to both Islam and Arabism. After Somalia, the new republic of Djibouti (which numbers few Arabs among its population) joined the Arab League (September 1977). The Comoros, which are Muslim but in which the

Arab segment of the populace, once significant, has
merged into a Swahili-speaking ethnic mix, have
also applied for membership (in July 1977), though
it has not yet been granted.

Latent conflicts exist between the Arab bloc and
other countries or groups that aspire to play a
similar role (most notably Iran), as well as countries
or peoples whose interests may suffer as a result of
increasing Arab power. Depending on how the
forces in the world line up, these conflicts may
either be smothered or fanned.

⤜ 4 ⤛
Prospects and Pitfalls for the Arab World

What role can the Arabs play in today's world? What are their prospects for tomorrow? Obviously, the answer to these questions depends in large part on the answer to another question: To what extent will they unite or remain divided?

Unifying and Differentiating Factors

As we have seen, Arabist ideology has pressed for unity. On the other hand, there have always been deep political divisions. What accounts for this twofold tendency?

There are, of course, deep reasons for the fact that the ideology of Arabism has taken Arab unity as its goal and that this choice has received such enthusiastic support. The most obvious unifying factor is the written language, the only language of culture, classical Arabic. The Arab countries also share a common history, particularly in its beginnings. The chivalric tales of the pre-Islamic Arabs, the rise of Islam in Arabia, shrouded in sacred aura, the heroic deeds of the conquerors, the glory and sumptuousness of the Damascus and Baghdad empires are riches in a treasure-house of memories that all Arabs have cherished through the ages.

Broadly speaking, the Arabs have always faced the same enemies—the crusaders and Mongols in the Middle Ages, European imperialism in the modern era—and they have always had the same ambiguous relations with the Turks. To some extent they share a common culture. This culture has continued the medieval Muslim cultural tradition, which was based on the Arabic tongue (in its intellectual aspects, at least) and so was often conceived of as an extension of pre-Islamic Arab culture and early Islam, enriched by many later contributions, most notably Iranian.

Many elements of this common culture are still alive, immediate, and active. Classical Arabic literature of the Middle Ages, though studied in school, no longer offers much to attract the modern reader. It is more respected than read but remains nonetheless a model of style and a vehicle of fundamental cultural values: moral, aesthetic, etc. Its most readily comprehensible elements, the innumerable anecdotes and maxims with which it is adorned, provide a frame of reference. The popular literature of the Middle Ages (chivalric stories and tales along the lines of the *Thousand and One Nights*), which the litterati held in deep contempt then as now, is still accessible and more eagerly read than the classics. Modern Arab literature, a product of the nineteenth century, is more readable. It has helped give wide currency to the ideas of the leading cultural circles.

Classical Arabic is not only a common literary language. It makes mutual communication and comprehension possible (through simplification and, frequently, compromise with the various dialects). Arabs who speak different dialects can understand one another perfectly in this tongue and can write so as to be understood anywhere in the Arab world. It is the language of political speeches, radio, and to some extent of the cinema and theater.

There are, moreover, important aspects of social life and many elements of daily culture (this time in the anthropological sense), customs, and collective mentalities that are to some degree shared.This is a vast area, very difficult to explore; to understand it, we would need a searching, detailed scientific study that would attempt to establish objective criteria. For the moment such studies are virtually nonexistent, and we must make do with literary surveys, both Arab and non-Arab, which sometimes reveal many interesting intuitions and much perspicacity and psychology understanding, but which fail to meet scientific criteria of verifiability. Here we shall refrain (we have no space in any case) from venturing too far onto this slippery ground (see chapter 5 below, however). We shall merely point out that some of the elements in question, which derive from medieval Muslim civilization or its common roots, are also found among non-Arab Muslim peoples, and on occasion even among non-Muslims.[1] Thus they cannot be regarded as specifically Arab.

Compared with these unifying factors, the fac-

1. Concerning familial customs, see, for example, Germaine Tillion, *Le harem et les cousins* (Paris: Seuil, 1966), with which I cannot agree entirely, particularly where the explanatory hypotheses are concerned, but which provides excellent descriptive material that clarifies a good many points.

tors of regional differentiation are no less striking. The various Arabized countries constitute economic regions, with all that that entails. In some cases a political unit corresponds roughly to at least a potential geographic and economic unit (Morocco, Tunisia, Egypt). In others the political unit does not correspond to a clearly defined geographic unit and has difficulty achieving economic unity. In any case, political boundaries have by now been successful in marking off zones within which networks of economic relations ensure that there will be a certain inherent unity and that common responses, aspirations, and interests will be able to form.

The language spoken in daily life varies from place to place. Infinite variations distinguish the speech of each village, each tribe, each city, and often each neighborhood. These variations are small, but their cumulative effect is large and gives rise to a group of related dialects in each region. Under modern conditions there is a tendency for these to coalesce.[2] Often the difference is greater between sedentary and Bedouin or urban and rural dialects in a given region than between dialects of different regions. Broadly speaking, the difficulties of comprehension increase with geographical or social distance. Modern life, however, as we shall show momentarily, has tended to bring these different linguistic forms closer together.

The mental outlook and daily customs and ac-

2. The term "accent," which has been used by some to minimize this phenomenon, is linguistically misleading; it refers to precisely this normal fragmentation of a language into different dialects.

tivities differ from region to region, as they differ
according to way of life, social class, and religious
affiliation. Each type of activity has its own boundaries, with some overlapping of different traits.
Each region also has its own history, before and
after Islam, before and after Arabization. Life in
the various regions is built on different substrates:
Berber and Latin in the Maghrib, Pharaonic and
Coptic in Egypt, Aramaic in the Fertile Crescent,
etc. These substrates often produce noticeable differences in the forms of life erected upon them.

Modern conditions sometimes seem to weigh in
favor of unity. Wide circulation of books and
newspapers, radio, television, movies, and increased ease of travel have made it possible for
Arabs living in widely separated areas to become
more familiar with one another. Mass education
has increased familiarity with the common classical
language in its modernized form. Even knowledge
of dialects other than one's own has been on the
rise. Everyone, for instance, knows at least the main
distinctive features of the urban Egyptian dialect,
thanks to the popularity of Egyptian films and
songs.

Weighing on the opposite side of the balance,
perhaps, are bureaucracy and other trappings of
the modern state.

If the bases of Arab unity do exist, the question
whether that potential is to be realized or the present division perpetuated will be decided less by the
underlying factors than by the balance of power
among existing states and political movements and
by possible external challenges calling for a more

or less unified response—in short, by historical circumstances. The same statement also applies to other politically divided but more or less culturally unified areas such as Europe, Black Africa, and Latin America; it was formerly true of the Greek cities of antiquity.

The most likely outcome is some degree of unification in certain areas. At present the order of the day is to overcome political divisions, at least in part; there are likely to be a good many ups and downs along the way to achieving this goal, including attempts at unification and, in their wake, separatist movements leading to secession, which may prove temporary and then again may not.

Resources

The Arab world is in possession of considerable resources. The member countries of the Arab League cover nearly 14 million square kilometers, or nearly twice the area of the United States (excluding Alaska and Hawaii). Counting only countries whose population is primarily Arab, when looked at from either a political or an ethnic point of view, we should be obliged to exclude Somalia and Djibouti (660,000 sq. km.), which would leave around 13,350,000 square kilometers.

The region boasts an impressive array of natural resources. "With only 3.1% of the world's population [the Arabs overall] possess a third of the world's proven reserves of phosphates and a large portion of world petroleum reserves, not to mention enormous resources in natural gas, copper, zinc, and coal, copper-bearing and potassium ores."[3] Iron in Mauritania and Algeria and manganese and lead in Morocco should also be counted. So much for underground resources. As for agricultural production, there are (long fiber) cotton in Egypt, Syria, and the Sudan, wood in the Sudan, and flax in Egypt. Human resources are abundant, of course, even overabundant under present conditions. But if mobilized in a well-designed development plan, this plentiful population could provide an adequate and useful supply of labor. There are skilled workers, though not in very large numbers; a program of professional training could increase the number of middle-level personnel, at present in particularly short supply. The potential internal market is sufficiently large to allow development of a self-contained economy.

The major weakness is in the area of food production. Only 20% of the land in the fifteen Arab countries can be cultivated, as compared with 47% in the United States. There is a crying lack of water. Despite some growth in agricultural production through expansion of the land area under cultivation and improvements in yield, agriculture in many Arab countries is still far from satisfying the rapidly increasing demand of a steadily growing population. These countries have had to resort to massive imports. Owing to the climate and the nature of the soil, considerable investment is necessary in order to create additional arable land and

3. Abdelkader Sid-Ahmed, *L'économie arabe à l'heure des surplus pétroliers* (Paris, 1975), p. 299 (= *Economies et Sociétés* 9, no. 3 (March 1975); = *Cahiers de l'ISMEA*, series F. no. 26, paginated 279–522). Much use has been made here of this remarkable synthesis.

increase yields. The result is an alarmingly precarious food supply and sporadic but undeniable malnutrition, with deficiencies particularly of animal protein.

It might be possible to remedy the inadequacy of the agricultural sector by carrying on with efforts to expand the area under cultivation and to increase yields. If scarcity persists, the Arab world has more than adequate finances to pay for the needed importation of foodstuffs. Now that Arab petroleum is being bought by the industrialized nations at a more reasonable price than was the case a few years ago, financing of these imports is no longer a problem, though this will remain true only for a limited period of time. If one adopts the Arab point of view, it becomes clear that the Arabs must take advantage of this petroleum rent as long as it lasts in order to eliminate or at least reduce their dependence on the outside world, to ensure sufficient advances in agricultural production, and to achieve an industrial development adequate to enable them to pay for their foreign purchases of food and other goods on a lasting basis.

To this potential in human, mineral, and vegetable resources we must add a geographical situation that offers numerous advantages. To be sure, it has offered, and no doubt continues to offer, a good many disadvantages as well. Proximity to industrialized Europe, a historical factor of great importance, is less important now than it was, in both positive and negative senses, thanks to speedier transportation. But the location of the region, between the advanced countries and Black Africa on the one hand, and Iran, India, and the Far East on the other—an unavoidable bridge between these areas—is just as important now as ever, both for good and for ill. On a whole range of vital problems, many countries must deal with the Arabs either as neighbors or as more distant partners. This makes mutual concessions a must, to say the least, and from this circumstance a modicum of unified leadership should be able to draw considerable advantage. In today's bipolar world, the Arab region has been like a turntable—able to hook itself on to a track leading to either of the great superpowers, whether their relations happened to be in a phase of conflict, competition, or "détente"; this has brought the Arabs much trouble, but they have also been able to make it pay, at times handsomely.

That natural handicaps have hampered the progress of the Arab world is undeniable. Mention has been made of those that have interfered with agricultural production. There is less variety in the mineral resources of the region than in other major regions or leading states. Systematic exploration of this potential is far from complete, however. A portion of the land that is barren today was once fertile but was abandoned to the desert, mainly for political or social reasons. But modern technology, providing it is backed by adequate financing, should be able to make up the ground lost and conquer new territory.

Prospects for Development

For the moment, only a small part of this potential has gone into development of a kind likely to bring a decent way of life, along with the full advantages, profits, and responsibilities of power, to all the inhabitants of the region.

This state of affairs is reflected in the still far from adequate progress of industrialization. While regular increases in the rate of growth (which has been quite high, moreover) have been registered during the last two decades, this overall progress has been the result of development of the extractive sector in a relatively small number of Arab countries.

Taken as a whole, the manufacturing sector is very weak. It produces few exportable goods. It requires little labor (like petroleum production). It contributes little to the modernization of other sectors. Its growth has been slow and has run up against a variety of obstacles. It consists mainly of light industries that transform agricultural raw materials for internal consumption: foodstuffs, textiles, construction, etc. Apart from producing necessary items of consumption, it has catered mainly to the tastes of the privileged upper classes.

Industry is unable to provide work for the enormous rural, or originally rural, population, which is dramatically underemployed. The percentage of the adult population included in the active work force is low. Underdeveloped agriculture absorbs far too high a proportion of the population. Illiteracy is widespread, and there are not enough skilled workers. Underdevelopment of higher education and research is a great handicap. It (along with other factors) is responsible for the "brain drain." According to UNESCO statistics, one-quarter of the "displaced brains" in the world are Arab. Thus thousands upon thousands of qualified individuals who, if properly utilized, could contribute greatly to the prosperity and progress of their own countries have left to add their talents to the riches of the developed countries. Similarly, some Arab countries lack an adequate labor supply and have even gone so far as to import workers from the non-Arab world (Turkey, Pakistan, etc.), while others have seen hundreds of thousands of their citizens emigrate to Europe.

It is legitimate to reject the European, American, and Soviet model of development through industrialization and to emphasize the kinds of distortion, alienation, and pernicious and disastrous consequences to which it leads. But underdevelopment gives rise to hunger, misery, catastrophe and suffering without limit. The peoples that endure these scourges can only hope for a kind of development that will afford them material well-being. No model is available to them but that of the industrial societies. The examples they see before them demonstrate that industrialization yields both greater prosperity and increased strength. They know that a nation unwilling to submit to the law laid down by more powerful nations must itself become powerful.

All the Arab countries have therefore chosen to proceed with industrialization, subject to the limitations imposed by the amount of available resources. But the degree of effort put into industrialization and the choice of sectors to be developed depend both on natural and social constraints and on governmental decision. These choices are contingent upon political options, both internal and external. The petroleum kingdoms of Arabia and the states in which the market economy predominates have chosen to develop their economies within the framework of the world capitalist economy. Structurally, this entails dependence on economic decisions made at the center of the system, within the most developed countries, and on the consequences thereof. This dependence is disguised and partially counterbalanced by spectacular results: the pressure that enormous petroleum revenues have made it possible to exert and the power thereby acquired to influence the system.

Such a choice can, of course, result in considerable growth, but it tends to give undue advantage to certain classes while doing nothing to remedy to wretchedness of the majority. Only in the tiny Gulf petroleum states have small populations made possible a broader distribution of the wealth. The alternative, to develop under a state capitalist system, makes it possible (in theory) to allocate resources more coherently, to plan investments more rationally, and to avoid the more glaring inequalities. But the smallness of the economic zone and the low initial level of development also enforce a high degree of foreign dependence. For the most part the aid of communist powers has been sought. This has made it easier for the states involved to exert some control over their dependence by maneuvering and manipulating coercive pressures from several "benefactor" countries, rather than deal with an uncoordinated variety of private interests. The "socialist" countries have discovered the possibility of making supervised and limited use of the services of capitalist firms. On the whole, however, dependence continues to exist.

At least at the present stage, genuine self-contained development and rational planning for the future would seem to require states to exert extensive control over their economies and to rule relatively extensive geographic areas. No Arab state is sufficiently large in this respect. Most of them are dramatically lacking in basic resources, while a few are choking on a glut of them. Here, economic necessities and pressures for increased prosperity converge with Arabist ideology. The best way to meet these requirements would be for the "poor" countries to join with the "rich." A wide-spread myth among the Arabs maintains that this union is hampered mainly by the maneuvers of the "imperialists." This is false, despite the involvement of the European powers in the division of the Fertile Crescent in 1920. It is in fact illusory to think that union can be achieved by joyful, willing sacrifice of what has been won on the altar of Arab fraternity (or even socialist internationalism), by voluntary renunication of the potential for exerting political control over the unification process on the part of present governments, and by spontaneous dissolution of ties of interest and local demands arising out of regional aspirations. At best ideology can produce limited forms of "aid." Most likely, deeper needs will make their force felt through inter-Arab struggles, which are likely to promote one or more Arab countries to a position of at least relative hegemony. Depending on what policies are adopted, the resulting political unit may ·achieve gradual consolidation of its constituent elements, or separatist demands may arise to impede such consolidation.

➤ 5 ◀

Is a Comprehensive Portrait of the Arabs Possible?

A book that attempts to give a survey of the Arabs should ideally include an analysis designed to bring out the general characteristics of their life, of their social behavior. As already mentioned, the dearth of detailed scientific studies means that adequate grounds for such an analysis are lacking. There is no shortage of works, by Arabs and others, many of them perceptive and intelligent, which attempt to make intuition serve where knowledge is lacking. The author of the present book has little taste or talent for work of this sort, though some of it is doubtless representative of reality in one degree or another. However, neither the fragmentary truths nor the stylistic brilliance sometimes found in these works can conceal the fact that the methods used are singularly subjective and based on precarious foundations. Generalization is difficult: it is not uncommon to see Western Arabs—when they are not merely critical—assume that their Eastern brothers behave just as they do (and vice versa). It is difficult to identify characteristics that are at once common to all Arabs and specific, i.e, not found among their neighbors. These difficulties, coupled with lack of space, compel us to limit our remarks to a few

rather commonplace generalities, which we trust
are less open to challenge than portraits of the sort
just alluded to, painted as they are with a very
broad brush.[1]

Structures of Production, Accumulation, and Distribution

Here as elsewhere, such structures play a very
important role, along with the level of wealth and
productivity, in shaping institutions and minds.
The organizers of the medieval world of Islam
forged a type of society many of whose characteristic aspects are still in evidence.

The most important forms of production were
agriculture and husbandry, carried on by settled
peasants in long-term symbiotic relationship with
nomadic shepherds. The basic production unit was
often communal (more or less egalitarian clans,
village communities), though usually there was a
privileged stratum. In general, surplus production
was confiscated either by a tribal aristocracy concentrated in a few ruling clans or by large landowners, who exacted tribute from small peasant
landowners (and they, in turn, sometimes exploited
"tenants" or hired laborers). This confiscation was
in general legitimated by the institution of private

1. Much can be gained by reading the weighty tome by C. A. O. Van
Niewenhuijze, *Sociology of the Middle East, a Stocktaking and Interpretation*
(Leiden: Brill, 1971), which contains an impressive bibliography. An
invaluable model of analysis of a particular region, couched in more
accessible form, is Pierre Bourdieu's *Sociologie de l'Algérie*, 2nd ed.
(Paris: Presses Universitaires Francaises, 1961), collection "Que
sais-je?," no. 802.

property, when it was not the result of coercion pure and simple.

The ruling class that ran the state accumulated considerable wealth, not only by confiscation of the surplus in the form of rent or tribute as well as tax, but also in booty from successful military campaigns and tribute paid by subjugated populations. This wealth was augmented by levies on industrial and in some cases agricultural production, whether by hired labor or slaves. With this wealth the ruling class, often residing in enormous cities, sustained an intermediate stratum of commercial craftsmen, merchants, officials, administrators, soldiers, intellectuals, artists, entertainers, etc.

Within this intermediate stratum the merchants played a role of considerable importance, distributing the products of agricultural, pastoral, and craft activities, which ultimately became highly specialized pursuits. They encouraged "international" trade on a vast scale and thereby shared in the surplus product generated outside the Islamic world. It is not certain that this external income had the crucial importance attributed to it by Samir Amin.[2] But the merchant class, which also profited by making loans, entered the ranks of the ruling class and imposed its values and cultural norms. Merchants frequently obtained property rights in the agro-pastoral sector as well. In part the merchant class organized production in this sector to serve its own interests. Unlike the European bourgeoisie,

2. Cf. Samir Amin, *La nation arabe, nationalisme et luttes de classes* (Paris: Editions de Minuit, 1976), pp. 14, 27 ff., 125 ff.

however, it never developed an important capitalist industrial sector.

From the eleventh century on, merchants were relegated to secondary status by the ascendancy of the military (whose ranks were often filled with slaves of foreign origin). Soldiers became land-owners, invested in commercial and industrial enterprises, and organized the state to their own advantage.

The productive surplus and the wealth in the hands of the ruling classes gradually diminished for a variety of reasons still not very well understood. The military class in power preferred present income to measures that the merchant bourgeoisie might have taken to foster organized growth of production and commercial profits. Wars and invasions destroyed much of the infrastructure of irrigation-dependent agriculture. The conquests came to a halt. Those made by the Ottoman Empire between the fourteenth and the seventeenth centuries brought little benefit to the subjugated Arab world. The location of the leading trade routes shifted to the detriment of the Islamic countries. The authoritarian organization of the guilds, particularly in the Ottoman era, discouraged possible initiatives on the part of commercial craftsmen.

Regional differences must be taken into account. In the Maghrib, for example, the dominant class was often molded by the aristocracy of nomadic tribes. Egypt has always produced a considerable agricultural surplus. But there was even greater variety from locality to locality and district to district. This highly various, complex palimpsest of structures makes it impossible to summarize the overall economic system of the medieval Muslim world, the Arab world, or even a broad subregion of the Arab zone in a handy formula (feudal mode of production, Asiatic mode, tributary mode, etc.). Nor can the evolution of that system be explained in terms of a simple dynamic law, as many Marxists would like to do (Marx's own prudence with regard to precapitalist economic formations notwithstanding).[3]

The general shrinking of resources impaired maintenance of the irrigation infrastructure and forced the rulers to increase their exploitation of the direct producers, which discouraged the latter from taking initiatives to improve the conditions of production.

With European industrial development, beginning in the late Middle Ages, Muslim craftsmen found that their products (most notably textiles) had to compete with lower-priced European goods. By the nineteenth century Europe's development had brought it sufficient economic, political, and military strength to enforce measures designed to foreclose any possibility of autonomous development in the Muslim East.

Capitalist structures have taken hold only to a limited degree. Exploitation of surplus production from the land is still managed largely through precapitalist structures. A landed aristocracy has maintained its hegemony over arable land, even

3. Cf. M. Rodinson, *Islam and Capitalism* (New York: Pantheon Books, 1973), pp. 58 ff., 61–68.

where some kind of agrarian capitalism has been able to make a start. Capitalist production, with its attendant industrial proletariat, is the moving force in a narrow sector, a peripheral appendage, as it were, of the central body of this type of economy, dependent on economic decisions taken at the center. All economic activity is in the grip of underdevelopment. The tertiary sector has swollen enormously and is largely parasitic.

Accentuated by external and internal forces presently at work, the weight of the past makes itself felt in the still overriding importance of the relation of landowner to "village hand," in the generalized dominance of the city, and in the perpetuation of commercial traditions. The efforts of the "socialist" states have been only partially successful in undoing these characteristics.

Ways of Life

Ever since prehistoric times people in this part of the world have chosen to live in ways determined primarily by natural conditions and by the level of productivity achieved. Later, however, social dynamics and political situations do influence the evolution and respective importance of these various ways of life.

At present, pastoralism, generally nomadic, which was the dominant way of life among pre-Islamic Arabs, is declining in importance and has lost the aristocratic prestige long associated with it. Still, the period of its flowering is often evoked as an ideal. In the countryside, settled villagers, who live by agriculture, are still numerically dominant but are held in relatively low esteem. City-dwellers top the status scale, but everywhere the centers of industrial civilization, with their enormous blocks of uniform and anonymous living cells, traversed by highways and surrounded by slums, are gaining ground over the traditional *madīna,* about which we shall next say a few words.

The Basic Social Unit

The family, the basic unit of all social relations, is everywhere found in its broad or extended form, of agnatic or patriarchal type. Grouped in an economic unit around the father, who is the leader, are his male descendants and their wives and children, living together in several nuclear families. There is a strong tendency to endogamy.

Filiation therefore follows the male line and women settle with the families of their husbands. This structure, characterized by masculine hegemony and concomitant subordination and confinement of women (with compensations in practice), has since before Islam been a very deeply rooted trait of culture throughout this part of the world, even among present-day Christian peoples living on the northern shores of the Mediterranean. But the Muslim populations have consecrated their customs by linking them to Islam, frequently going beyond the prescriptions laid down by the Koran. These features are not all found in every Arabized population, some of them being absent among the Berbers, for example. Nor, apparently, were they prevalent among all pre-Islamic Arab tribes, some of which were ruled by

women;[4] some authors have interpreted certain
facts about these tribes as indicative of "matriar-
chy."

Under modern conditions the extended family
has tended to give way to the nuclear family, which
has made for increased individual autonomy and a
more positive role for women. Once kept strictly
apart outside the home, the two sexes are now beginning to mingle somewhat. The extent of this
development, however, varies from place to place,
and on the whole remains rather limited.

Basic forms of the larger society

The tribe and the village, and to some degree
also the city or city quarter, are the basic units in
which the social life of men and women unfolds,
linking together smaller groups organized around
specific functions.

Found in a variety of sizes, these clans, segments,
etc., are linked together in a comprehensive structure expressed in terms of kinship, each unit trac-
ing its origins back to a common ancestor supposedly related to the ancestors of other similar
units. Segments sometimes split off from the main
group and form alliances. Each group consists of
related individuals who may attach "clients" or dependents to themselves. Found in their purest
form among the nomadic shepherds, these units

---

4. In the fourth century a Christian author generalized thus: "It is
said that women reign over them [the Arab]"; cf. *Expositio totius mundi
et gentium*, ed. J. Rougé (Paris: Editions du Cerf, 1966, sec. 20, pp. 154
ff. ("Sources chrétiennes," no. 124).

also include peasants and sometimes city-dwellers in certain regions. Only with difficulty can the pastoral tribes forgo the services of cities, most notably as marketplaces.

Isolated dwelling places are relatively rare in the countryside. The village is a microcosm that tends toward autarchy. Once concerned with the village only in order to exploit it, the state is now seeking to integrate village life into the larger society, with incomplete success. Often the village structure persists, sometimes with a split into two rival factions and a more or less clandestine leader, on which the authorities impose their official representative.

Cities have played a very important role, though in general without attaining the level of autonomous political development achieved by Greek or medieval Western cities. The major institutions of the classic Muslim city are the great mosque, in which the faithful gather for prayer on Fridays, with social and political as well as religious significance; the *hammām*, or public bath, which is an extension of the public baths of antiquity, and the market (*sūq*), a place for trade between the local craftsmen and people from the surrounding countryside and other cities. Center of communication and cultural diffusion, linchpin of the distribution network, the traditional city comprised several quarters, each walled like the city itself and equipped with its own governors. These quarters grouped together people of similar ethnic or geographical origin or religious affiliation and, more than the city, served as basic building blocks of the larger society. The city's unity was ensured, however, by the existence of mixed quarters and common institutions: a central *sūq*, a *muḥtasib*, who was both provost of the merchants and moral censor, religious guilds and confraternities, and the official representative of the central authorities, the Muslim judge (*qāḍī*). The modern city, which at first rose alongside the traditional city, has gradually absorbed and transformed it.

The Encompassing Social Units

Ever since the dawn of history these various basic units have entered into more or less close relations with others of their kind. Based on perceived cultural and linguistic unity, ideologized in myths of common origin and ancient cults, and characterized by certain common institutions, such relations were subjected to tight control or domination by states ruled by one element or another, which had somehow obtained power over the rest. During the period of universalist religions, the unifying role of language and culture was partially supplanted by the community of faith. This ideology was institutionalized as the cement of the state edifice. Hegemony was granted to one faith in a context of confessional pluralism.

Structures very like states—resembling the true South Arabian states and capable of temporarily imposing limits on the restless independence of the tribes, especially in the outlying regions—were known among the Arabs before Islam. They were called "kingdoms" (*mulk*) and were essentially political structures, though in some cases a central cult provided additional ideological mortar. Important neighboring states were occupied by the Arabs after they became Muslims; the Sassanid Empire in Persia and the Byzantine Empire. The Arabs adopted many of their institutions. State religions (Zoroastrianism, Christianity) and outbreaks of intolerance notwithstanding, these states allowed other religious communities to exist and afforded them considerable independence. Even their hegemonic churches had their own hierarchy, parallel to that of the state but not identical with it.

The fact that the Muslim religion developed initially in a stateless tribal society led Muḥammad to establish a politico-religious community, which was based on faith as the criterion of membership but which subjected believers to the authority of a political structure. Subsequent evolution was conditioned by the complex relations between this new structural principle and earlier political structures. The "successors" or "lieutenants" (*khalīfa,* caliph) of the Prophet were in principle both leaders of the Muslim community (*amīr al-mu'minīn,* prince of believers) and of the conquering Arab state, which were initially identified. The state was supposed to be governed in accordance with the laws of the community, and the Ummayad dynasty (650–750) was accused of having flouted this principle by transforming the caliphate (*khilāfa*) into a "kingdom" (*mulk*).

In practice many Byzantine and Sassanid institutions continued to function, and Islam itself

was tolerant of other monotheistic religions like
Christianity and Judaism, which were held to contain the main tenets of the true doctrine, though in
more or less distorted form. They retained considerable autonomy under the authority of the Muslim state. Its rapid disintegration gave rise to regional states, which were secular in the sense that
they no longer recognized the political authority of
the caliph over their territory. Religious schisms
also led to the creation of competing politico-
religious structures.

Accordingly, where Islam was dominant (*dār al-
Islām*, "the home of Islam") each family and each
larger social unit had a place within a common
cultural milieu, but each was at the same time subject to an officially Muslim state and part of a religious community that might be hegemonic or subordinate, and even in some cases (Muslim dissidents, for example) illegal. For subordinate
groups (Christians and Jews) primary allegiance
went to the community, not the state, though frequently they were tied by practical or even emotional ties to the ruler, who tended to favor these
"protected peoples" when it suited his purpose,
and who as the upholder of law and order had to
defend them against violent outbursts by the Muslim mob when the privileges accorded these un-
believers proved too much for it. Sometimes this
"tolerance" gave way to pressure from the masses
or to the excessive zeal of a monarch. Furthermore,
the Christians had a tendency to look to states
where they were in power (Europe, Byzantium) or

influential (Mongols), much as the heretical Muslims did. The Jews took advantage of the tolerance while it lasted and took in Jewish victims of Christian persecution, but they could feel no real ties to a state capable at times of inciting persecution against them.

The "orthodox" Muslim, for his part, recognized a duty of loyalty to the state, but only if the state was the legitimate organization of the community that religious law held it must be. Otherwise the regime constituted a form of "oppression" (*zulm*) that could legitimate rebellion. Loyalty thus went more to the ideal than to the real state, and, apart from some "heretics," no one invoked any external standard of comparison.

In the nineteenth century the popularity of the European model of the nation-state gradually but incompletely altered the traditional relations between state and confession. First of all, the Ottoman Empire (which included most of the Arab countries), was moving toward that model, though with much hesitation and backsliding, and did much in this period to overcome confessional isolation in the Near East.[5] But it differed from the European norm by its multiethnic character and the hegemony of the Turkish element. In the Maghrib and Arabia, the absence of Christians led to an identification of the Muslim confession with the Arab ethnos. Arabic-speaking Jews in these regions sacrificed their Arabhood. In Algeria, where

5. See especially the admirable book by Niyazi Berkes, *The Development of Secularism in Turkey* (Montreal: McGill University Press, 1964).

the Crémieux decree made them naturalized
Frenchmen, they gave their allegiance to the culture of the French. More generally, the Zionist
movement formulated in the name of Arabic-
speaking Jews a claim to their own nationality.

As we have seen, the evolution of the Arab states
away from dependence on religious underpinnings
has been limited. Since 1920 the political and
juridical influence of confessional structures has
been particularly strong in Lebanon and Palestine.
Confessional structures were institutionalized in
these areas owing to the political influence of
foreign powers (France and Britain), defensive reactions on the part of the Christian communities,
fear on the part of Shiites and Druze of a renewal
of their traditional subjugation by the Sunnite
Muslims, whose full support for secular principles
they doubted, and finally in consequence of Zionist
aims.

Today the Arab states are only partly nation-
states. To be sure, they benefit from "regional"
feelings of patriotism, sometimes very deeply
rooted (as in Egypt, Morocco, etc.), and from networks of interest and aspiration such as all states
foster. But Arabist ideology has encouraged the
belief that a nation-state can be fully legitimate only
if it includes all Arabs. The strength of confessional
ties, the interests and aspirations of classes, international ideologies, tribal structures where they
persist, and in some cases the non-Arab characteristics of minority groups (most notably language) all reinforce the feeling that the existing

states are only temporary and so reduce the force of allegiance to them.

Consciousness of Social Stratification

Nationalism always tends to minimize the importance of the division of society into classes. In this respect Arab nationalism has been reinforced by Muslim ideology, according to which the community of the faithful embodies the egalitarian ideal.

It is nevertheless beyond doubt that a hierarchy of social strata (certainly different from the classes of industrial society) did exist in medieval Muslim societies. Of this fact people were fully conscious; the term "class" (*ṭabaqa*) was known, and some medieval authors attempted to give it a precise meaning.[6]

Individuals generally let their awareness of belonging to one stratum or another—an uncertain awareness with little ideological character—take second place to religious ideologies, to ideologies of multiclass communities. The ideal was peaceful and equitable coexistence of the various classes, which was supposed to be achievable by strict appli-

6. Cf. M. Rodinson, "Histoire économique et histoire des classes sociales dans le monde musulman," *Studies in the Economic History of the Middle East,* M. A. Cook, ed. (London: Oxford University Press, 1970), pp. 139–55. Many works could be added to those on classes that I cited, most notably the classification of the "sections" of the Egyptian people by Maqrīaī (d. 1442) in his *Treatise on Famines.* A lengthy documentation on this subject has been compiled by I. M. Lapidus, *Muslim Cities in the Later Middle Ages* (Cambridge, Mass.: Harvard University University Press, 1967), pp. 79 ff.

cation of religious law, most notably Islamic law. During the struggle for independence this ideal was bolstered by the national ideal, and liberty, invested with every virtue, was by itself supposed to bring about the same result.

Limited industrialization and independence gave rise to truly ideological class consciousness expressive of a will to power. This consciousness was at first slow to form, however, because national aspirations (economic autonomy, irredentism) remained unsatisfied and community-based ideologies (particularly in Lebanon), which were influenced both by class factors (partial coincidence of divisions among classes and divisions among communities) and by national factors (related to real or imagined, past and sometimes present compromises between certain communities and foreign powers), were perpetuated and even revived.

The present—probably temporary—situation is consequently a tangled web of class-, community-, and nation-based ideologies. The nationalist "socialism" invoked by several Arab states has created a partly novel stratification, the reality of which official ideology refuses to recognize. The result is repression of the class consciousness of the emerging classes. Stratification, with nothing very special about it, does nonetheless exist now as before, and it cannot fail to produce its usual effects.

Knowledge and Manipulation of the World

Among the medieval Arabs we find the usual systems of knowledge and action common to societies at this stage: empirical technology and science, theoretical science, occult sciences, philosophy, and rational theology (*kalām*). Initially, at any rate, we encounter nothing specifically Arab except in the forms of knowledge connected with analysis of the Muslim ideological corpus (Koran, Tradition of the Prophet, etc.), couched in the Arabic tongue, along with learning related to analysis of that language itself. In large part, however, this scholarship was the work of specialists of non-Arab origin, whose everyday language was not Arabic.

Science and philosophy made advances that often showed great originality and brilliance, building mainly on Greek concepts and achievements, though Iranian and Indian contributions were also important. Today, European and American science and technology, objectively the most advanced in the world, are being assimilated and put to use. Arab contributions to this body of knowledge will add to the general stream of scientific and technological progress. The scientific legacy of the Muslim Middle Ages, which once served as a guide to Europe, is now obsolete. Only vestiges remain in certain popular practices and sayings and in the minds of some members of the clergy with particularly archaic leanings.

Ideological Consciousness

Arabs, then, have been coming more and more to view the natural world through science and technology, just as others have done. Of society and culture, however, their views are at once more distinctive and more various.

In one degree or another society and culture are

seen in the light of certain supreme, transcendent values, demanding total devotion from all individuals. These values determine general goals desirable for all, and serve to focus the interests and aspirations that grow out of everyday experience.

If we neglect minority religious ideologies, we come first to current Muslim ideology, at the moment the only ideology in the Arab world to be based on a definite corpus of ideas and practices. An object of worship, this corpus is still used as a standard of reference, even if large parts of it are unfamiliar to most. The tie to Islam, which is felt by virtually everyone and is stronger than the attachment to God, is a sense of belonging, a pride in a community (*umma*) that is distinguished from the rest of mankind by a superior ideal, set forth by an exceptional man, the prophet Muḥammad. Though particular items of dogma are often unfamiliar or totally ignored and there is great unevenness in the observation of ritual, there is continuing widespread acceptance of the fundamental dogma of a God (Allāh), remote ruler of a creation wholly subject to his will, who requires men to lead a moral life (and administers punishment if they do not). It is virtually impossible to repudiate this dogma openly.

The divine origin of Muḥammad's inspiration is often passed over in silence or in any case given little prominence. In general he is regarded as a leader, an Arab superpatriot, endowed with great virtue, unifier and guide of the nation as well as founder of a singularly just and harmonious social system.

Often, allegiance to Islam, which is usually thought of as a nationalist sentiment, a religious patriotism, goes hand in hand with loyalty to a superior system of social values. These values are those of the traditional world, which is idealized as a world in which the pace of life was calm and tranquil. Other supreme social values are a will to justice and goodness, tempered by the firmness made necessary by human imperfection; total sexual reserve on the part of women; and, for men, reserve within the limits of their supposedly irresistible sexual instincts; and so forth. If traditional Muslim society did not altogether exemplify these values, as is sometimes reluctantly acknowledged, the problem lay with the misfortunes of the time, with human nature, and above all with the perfidy of non-Muslims. Along with the Europeans (crusaders in the past, colonialism in the modern world) and the Mongol hordes, despised by all Muslims, the Arabs also blame the immoral Iranians and the brutal, conquering Turks, even though they are Muslims.

The personal goal that was paramount for traditional Islam, namely, the quest for salvation in the other world, has thus given way to overriding temporal goals: creation of a just community, a requirement laid down by Islam at its inception, and Arab greatness, which used to be not an object of theory but a mere transitory practical end, dissimulated and even repressed in Muslim consciousness.

If Muslims in general are ready to invoke Islam as a sanction for their opposition to the values of

industrial society, held to embody both immorality
and treason to the nation, the "bourgeoisie" (including the "new class" in the so-called socialist
states) is preaching fidelity to the Muslim moral
code as a bulwark of conservatism. The dispossessed masses, on the other hand, invoke the
Muslim code as a goal, as a sanction for their opposition to the inequality and exploitation that they
believe it condemns.

The second major ideological tendency is the
true religion of our time, nationalism. In contrast
to Islam, it has no basic corpus of authoritative
texts. But a few quite simple ideas, based on widespread forms of social behavior, have been
sufficient to give a decisive orientation to consciousness and action. Among these we find the
usual nationalist myths, modified to fit the case of
the ethnonational group. The Arab nation is "vouchsafed an eternal mission" (in the words of Michel
'Aflaq, the Christian theoretician of the Ba'th
party); it has always willed the Good and always
been the innocent victim of the wickedness of other
peoples. Its real past exploits (political, military,
and cultural) are exalted, sometimes with exagger-
ation, and no cloud is ever allowed to darken the
horizon. Present-day nationalist concepts are pro-
jected onto the past. The real connection between
the Arab people and Islam has been used to enable
the Arabs to take credit for most, if not all, of the
achievements of Muslims in general, and to enable
Arabs to lay claim to all the Muslim virtues. Thus a
link has been forged between Arabist and Muslim
ideology. Similarly, as has been the case with other

universalist ideologies, it is assumed that the goals of the Arab nation can only be beneficial for all mankind. Such an assumption can achieve positive results when it is used to guide action rather than to sanctify it after the fact.

Socialist ideology, also universalist, is widespread, too, particularly since the concept of socialism is quite vague and open to various interpretation. The term in fact connotes an aspiration to solidarity and hostility to "undeserved" privilege. Implicit in its use is opposition to European and American capitalism, or at least to the excesses of imperialism, which opposition no one can blame. It is widely held that the values sanctioned by Islam, including those Islamic values supposedly derived directly from Arab customs, are "socialist."

Reflected in various ways by individuals and groups, these three ideological tendencies can be interpreted in conservative ways as well as given a reformist or revolutionary tinge. While religion and nationalism have been preached to promote unity against internal protest, they have also been used to lead the masses in struggles against foreign domination and may sanction attacks on social strata or structures held to be unfaithful to religious or nationalist ideals. Socialism is more likely to foster opposition, but it can also be used to disparage opposition in states supposedly involved in the building of socialist society.

Models of Daily Behavior

Even a vaguely defined ideological system lays it down that the individual should dedicate his daily existence to the achievement of a great ideal: a harmonious Muslim society consistent with the vision of the Koran, a united and independent nation, a society without undeserved privileges. As a result, everyone in the society chooses a personal ideology for himself. These individual ideologies incorporate elements that have received little or no theoretical treatment, being derived, rather, from past or present social practice. By such a process ideal models are built up. Individualistic models come into competition with other models associated with religious belief, patriotism, or socialism. Individualist ideologies enter into compounds with systematic ideologies in very complex and contradictory ways, which vary from person to person and situation to situation. Personal interests and aspirations, along with deep-seated anthropological instincts, are set down alongside broader criteria and impose a style of their own on the more systematic ideas.

One such model is perhaps the main legacy of the pre-Islamic Arabs to today's Arab world. It lays down an image to which an individual must conform if he wishes a high place in a status hierarchy. What is involved is the "honor" (*'ird*) of the individual or small group. Some have maintained that, more than the cult of the gods, the cult of honor was the real religion, the real social bond, of pre-Islamic Arabia.[7] As the social units of that society were permanently at war, the notion of honor included strength, material or moral power. It im-

7. Edouard (Bichr) Farès, *L'honneur chez les Arabes avant l'Islam, étude de sociologie* (Paris: Adrien-Maisonneuve, 1932).

plied courage, the capacity and the will to defend the independence of the group and the chastity and freedom of its women and dependents, readiness to avenge insults, generosity, and hospitality. The group had to be fortunate in war and needed to have many sons, wise leaders capable of exercising their power with discretion, and gifted poets and orators, able to compete "honorably" in verbal jousts (*mufākharāt*) in which each tribe and clan rivaled the others in "boasting." A man must "honor" his word; to do so was a sign of strength. Loss of honor, shame, or debasement was a terrible punishment.

This Arab cult of honor, which fosters a rebellious, arrogant, often anarchic individualism (of the small group), was perpetuated after Islam and even spread more widely, for the Arabized peoples shared similar values. The Prophet, however, had sought to subordinate the code of honor to another moral code, that is, to rationalize all behavior with service of God and piety as the exclusive goals. The Prophet's goals implied, among other things, an emphasis on humility, on renunciation of vengeance and power.

Islam was no more successful than Christianity or Buddhism in completely imposing its moral code on people who converted to the faith. Yet the effectiveness of its ethical outlook was heightened by a quite different system of values which in some respects paralleled that of Islam. Widespread among both rural and urban Islamized peoples, who for millennia had been subjects of despotic states, this ethical system placed a high value on resignation and submission to the established order. The historical Muslim states had no choice but to adopt the oppressive and exploitative structures of these states, despite their ambition to establish an egalitarian community of believers, ultimately subject only to God. Beginning in the eleventh century, Islam was broken up and dismembered by numerous revolutionary schisms provoked by groups fighting to achieve their egalitarian ideal, which led to an authoritarian reaction. The state's means for exercising repression and coercion were strengthened and refined, and orthodoxy was strictly defined and inculcated by a new educational system.

Sunnism, the name for this essentially conservative orthodoxy, called upon the faithful to respect authority and the Muslim tradition as it had been laid down in the third century of the Hegira (ninth century A.D.), together with the customs that had been incorporated in that tradition and sanctified by being linked to the oral teachings of the Prophet. In a classic manner, submission to order and custom were laid down as corollaries of obedience to God.

Neither in spirit nor in act, however, was this submission ever complete. Thanks to the weakness of the administrative and law-enforcement apparatus, there was extreme decentralization, and social units at the grass roots enjoyed great independence; in Arabia, Berberdom, and elsewhere, tribal structures continued to dominate. The state was thus opposed by independent groups. It is true that these were equally as traditionalist as the state itself, if not more so, but their deliberately anarchic unruliness could well encourage the expression of opposition. The desire to see establishment in practice of the equality among believers promised by God gave rise to protest movements against the prevalent iniquities, as well as to many individual acts of protest. Mysticism sometimes gave direction to the latter and brought the individual into a personal relationship with God which could not fail to inspire disdain for the official version of what the divine will was.

Thus two distinct and partly contradictory orientations coexisted and continue to coexist, one looking to order, the other to individual expression. Modern conditions have strengthened both tendencies and have sometimes added new features to them, but no dialectical synthesis has managed to fuse the two. At most the two attitudes have combined to foster an often unconscious inclination on the part of the privileged members (even those with revolutionary views) of a highly stratified society to enjoy their privileges with a minimum of guilt and a maximum of pleasure, and to look upon the cultural and social inferiority of the disadvantaged strata as natural. Aristocratic proclivities (also present among many other peoples) are the result. A noteworthy consequence of this state of affairs has been an alarming persistence of the tendency to disparage manual labor.

Symbolism

Perhaps one should look for a genuine Arab specificity—a set of distinctive features found in the

Arabs and only in the Arabs—at the level of systems of signs, or symbols. Such symbols have an efficacity and emotional charge of their own; they represent social practices and social structures, ideologies, and systems of norms and values.

We are unable to enlarge upon this theme, owing to the lack of a sufficient number of thorough and detailed studies, the complexity of the problem, and insufficient space. We shall merely set down the working hypothesis that the common use of Arabic, the fund of oral traditions spread by the language, and the prestige afforded the Arabian Arabs as the founders of Islam must all have contributed to the creation of a specifically Arab symbolism of some sort.

It has frequently been suggested that it was less symbolism itself than the important role played by symbols in the life of the Arabs that was distinctive. Much stress has been laid in particular on Arab liking for rhetoric and lack of concern for the relation between words and concrete facts. The specificity of this tendency needs to be examined more closely, however, and some means of measuring it established. Such a tendency may well have been fostered by the structure of the Arabic tongue and the prestige of poetry in the history of Arabic literature. But the reported difference between Arabs and other people might be related (at least in part) to a more general phenomenon, the gap between aspirations and realistic possibilities of achieving them, even if it does surely find expression in a specifically Arab key.

Aesthetic Values

The traditional Arab aesthetic sensibility derives from the fusion of a number of ancient Middle Eastern artistic traditions, which took place during the Hellenistic era, with an appreciable infusion of Greek influence (quite apparent in the Arabian peninsula itself, particularly among the pre-Islamic South Arabians) and of Iranian influence. During the Islamic era this ancient Middle Eastern substrate was partly purged of forms to which the prestige of Hellenic culture had given wide currency for a millennium. Some of the diverse traditions of which the substrate was composed reflected the repugnance felt by some (though not nearly all) groups for figurative representation of animate creatures. A similar origin accounts for the strength of this repugnance in Judaism, as well as for the resurgence of iconoclasm in the Byzantine Empire. Though abstention from such representations in Islam was far from complete, it did contribute greatly to the tendency to prefer forms such as arabesque and calligraphy in the plastic arts.

Within the Muslim world the region in which this repugnance was greatest (though by no means exclusive) may have coincided more or less with the zone in which Arabic was spoken. This coincidence may be a consequence of the fact that this was precisely the zone in which the iconophobic traditions were strongest before Arabization and Islamization. Then, too, we must consider that the strong Iranian iconographic tradition was there less in-

fluential, though it did play some part because
of the appreciable mingling of different ethnic
groups and the high mobility of artisans throughout the Muslim world. Perhaps most important is
the fact that this was the area where the legalistic
religious tradition was most strictly observed.[8] An
index of the importance of this factor may be seen
in the fact that figurative realism flourished in
Egypt during the period (tenth to twelfth centuries) when the Fātimid heresy within the Shī'ite
tendency held sway there.[9]

This traditional sensibility has been profoundly
shaken during the last two centuries by the prestige
of European art. All of its forms have influenced
Arab artists and craftsmen. Kitsch has had the
greatest influence on the "bourgeoisie" and has
even reached the masses. More recently, higher
forms of art have affected elite circles, sometimes
resulting in straightforward adoption of European
forms, but also inspiring in some cases happy
syntheses with indigenous traditions. The
nonfigurative tradition has, moreover, been re-
habilitated by the evolution of European art itself.
From elite circles outward, a broader transformation of sensibility is taking shape, which has avoided
rejecting of the legacy of the past outright.

The traditional taste in music was also formed by
a synthesis of ancient Oriental, Hellenic, and Arabian Arab traditions. During the Middle Ages it

8. Cf. J. Sourdel-Thomine, "Peinture arabe et société musulmane,"
Revue des études islamiques 31 (1963):115–21; "Art et société dans le
monde de l'Islam," ibid., 36 (1968):93–114.

9. Cf. R. Ettinghausen, "Early Realism in Islamic Art," *Studi orien-
talistici in onore di G. Levi della Vida* (Rome, 1956), vol. 1, pp. 250–73.

exerted some influence on Western music, which in part shared similar origins with the music of the East and in some respects resembled it rather closely. Here again, the influence of the West, where the evolution of music followed a different course, has been strong for the past two centuries. The Arabs have nevertheless remained deeply attached to their own tradition. To be sure, some elements of European music have worked their way into song, but they have been integrated in a synthesis that bears a predominantly Arab stamp. In music it might be possible to identify a fairly distinctive unity, despite the constant intermingling of Persian, Turkish, Arab, and other elements, as well as wide regional variations.[10]

The National Character

In the public mind—prescientific or precritical—there has always been an idea of a "character" associated with each ethnic group or nation, based on the idea of the character of an individual. This group character has been regarded as an eternal essence associated with each people, and has been tainted by value judgment. When a group expresses its opinion of other groups, it generally takes its own (idealized) behavior as a norm and brands any behavior that deviates from that norm as "defective."[11]

It is no doubt true that the conditions of life and

10. Full details will be found in the invaluable synthesis of Simon Jargy, *La musique arabe* (Paris: Presses Universitaires Françaises, 1971), coll. "Que sais-je?" no. 1436. *A History of Arabian Music to the Thirteenth Century* (London: Luzac and Co., 1929).

11. Cf. M. Rodinson, "Racisme et ethnisme," *Pluriel* 3 (1975):7–27.

the social norms of each group have historically imposed on the members of that group more or less enduring attitudes and forms of behavior. Consider, for example, the influence that the special characteristics of sexual life in the Muslim countries cannot fail to exert. On the other hand, it is by no means certain that there is any significance to the proportion of members of each group who react to external stimuli in one manner or another (primary or secondary repercussions, propensity to activity, to emotivity, etc.)—and these reactions are the basis of individual character. These styles of reaction must in some degree depend on physiological structures, whose distribution may not have any relation with the ethnonational groups.

At this point we possess no ethnic character definitions of the Arabs based on scientific research. Typological studies of this sort have touched on groups within the Arab world too small and too disparate to allow any conclusions to be drawn. Apart from the great difficulty of giving such characterizations of any people, there are further problems in the Arab case due the wide dispersion of the people, who have settled in regions of rather various character with different histories, social structures, and natural endowments. The popular ethnic characterology that Arabs themselves express in a wealth of maxims and aphorisms distinguishes between the character of the Egyptians and that of the Syrians, between the Tunisians and the Moroccans, between the Yemenis and the Arabian Bedouins, etc. This oral literature maintains, no doubt rightly, that different "characters" stem from different ways of life. There is probably some truth in these empirical judgments, as well as in the attempts at synthesis that have been made both Arab and non-Arab authors, with varying degrees of caution.

One of the most serious and penetrating essays of this kind is that of the Tunisian historian and essayist, Hichem Djaït, which I shall summarize as an instructive example.[12] He attempts to apply to the Arab case the principles laid down by Kardiner and his colleagues for studying the "basic personality." In particular, he is concerned to define the basic personality of the contemporary Tunisian, and he is careful to place appropriate stress on the historical vicissitudes of the evolution of that personality. But he believes that, with slight shadings and a few corrections, his portrait can be extended to all of the Maghrib. In the Arab East similar models with various leading characteristics have been proposed.

According to the elaborate analyses of H. Djaït (for which I leave him the responsibility), the most prominent aspects of the basic Arab personality are the following: a "strong affectivity," which is repressed by society but ill-disciplined; a deep narcissism; an anxious search for the approval of others, strongly emphasizing status values based on appearances; and, finally, aggressiveness, directed toward different objects and expressed in a variety of ways.

Day-to-day observation may in many cases seem

12. H. Djaït, *La personnalité*, pp. 195–228.

to confirm the features of this unindulgent portrait. Our Tunisian author makes those features even more harsh by his severity toward "Levantine (urban) man, who lacks firmness and combativeness, lives on hollow grandeur, and yet is refined and cultivated" (p. 222). Still, it is also possible to find many individuals with characters that at first sight would seem to contradict at least some of the features of this analysis. Mr. Djaït gives extensive explanations of characteristics he believes to be attributable to the early education of the child. Apparently, the common way of fondling the small male child, spoiled by the hovering females of the family, is not without pernicious consequences.

Despite the impression that may be left by the assertions just summarized, Mr. Djaït is not guilty of neglecting the influence of institutional and social structures. It should be noted, further, that he emphasizes deep-seated characteristics masked by the tendencies he describes. This being the case, he writes, "a radical reform of the fundamental social institutions [in Kardiner's sense] could bring considerable changes. New adaptations will occur and will bring about a revolution in the economy of the self. What can and should remain is a deep core, a way of envisaging interpersonal relations, a way of confronting pleasure and pain, life and death. The Arab man might then liberate himself from his sexual fantasies, from his anxiety, from his narcissism, from his pomposity, all of which are experienced as an *adventitious protective covering of the Self,* and yet remain generous, resigned with that noble resignation [to the inevitable, which also gives rise to calm courage in action], sensitive to the approval of others, warm, spontaneous within reasonable limits, and quick to respond to the call of *muruwwa* [the ideal of nobility and humanity], of solidarity, and of communal brotherhood" (p. 224).

For now, one can do no more than record these observations and note carefully the ways in which they agree and disagree with the thousand facets of concrete individual behavior. Until further research and thorough scientific syntheses have been completed, the only way to avoid being taken in by appearances ultimately drawn from the well of ideology, whether apologetic or hostile, is to adopt a wait-and-see attitude on this particularly delicate subject.

➤ Conclusion ◀

Ever since the Islamic expansion more than thirteen centuries ago, the Arab world and Europe have frequently been locked in conflict. Such a state of affairs is common between neighboring peoples and is the rule when they subscribe to rival political ideologies. As is also the rule in such cases, this has resulted in each group's judging the other more on the basis of the state of relations between them at any given moment than on the basis of objective observation. The hatred and contempt of both sides for the rival religious ideology have been supplanted by contempt for the vanquished people on one side, and by hatred of the oppressor on the other. Further complex developments have recently set off a wave of anti-Arabism in Europe and particularly in France. The Arabs have looked upon themselves—and have been looked upon by the "critical West," in A. Laroui's phrase—as essentially a victimized people. This self-judgment has given rise, not unexpectedly, to an apologetic outlook that the observer may often find irritating.

It is not our intention that reservations imposed by scientific caution as to the specific general characteristics of the Arab world, or skepticism as to certain Arab nationalist myths, should be taken as signs of indifference to anti-Arabism. Nor have we shut our eyes to the crushing weight of traditions exalted by nationalists despite their pernicious consequences, to the undue obsession with political objectives, to the ascendancy of ideologies that inspire extremist and uncritical support, or to the hypocrisy in the behavior of the old and new bourgeoisies. In time of struggle nationalism inevitably finds expression in ways marred by a disagreeable note of self-satisfaction and apology.

But these are normal and usually transitory phenomena that have arisen many times in similar situations with other peoples, though they are often forgotten once the situation has faded into the past. These manifestations are largely the result of conditions imposed on the Arabs against their will. It would be easy to show that those who are most critical of such attitudes in the Arabs not only generalize unduly but are also far from innocent themselves; they are at the very least socially and historically linked to structures that have contributed to forming the attitudes they criticize.

Whenever the battle reaches fever pitch, second- or third-rate ideologists come to the fore, eager to exploit the situation for material advantage or status. Like the members of the ruling strata, whose primary concern is to protect their own interests, they hide from the eyes of outside observers the masses of workers, researchers, and artists, intellectuals, and dedicated and disinterested political activists, who live and work in difficult conditions. Whether the attitudes and behavior of

Arab societies are specific, regional, or more broadly based, these societies have produced in the past, and are producing today, works (in the broadest sense) of high quality. They have contributed much of great value to the common patrimony of human culture. The Arabs have exhibited and do exhibit qualities worthy of high esteem. In daily intercourse many of them display much humanity, intelligence, sensitivity, and benevolence. Though no people is to be admired wholly and uncritically or supported unconditionally in all its undertakings, the Arabs' historical cultural has on balance shown itself worthy of the esteem of all mankind; its legitimate objectives (or what is legitimate in its objectives) should command support and solidarity.

➤ Index ◄